The Seafarers THE VIKINGS

Other Publications:

PLANET EARTH
COLLECTOR'S LIBRARY OF THE CIVIL WAR
LIBRARY OF HEALTH
CLASSICS OF THE OLD WEST
THE EPIC OF FLIGHT
THE GOOD COOK
THE ENCYCLOPEDIA OF COLLECTIBLES
THE GREAT CITIES
WORLD WAR II
HOME REPAIR AND IMPROVEMENT
THE WORLD'S WILD PLACES
THE TIME-LIFE LIBRARY OF BOATING
HUMAN BEHAVIOR
THE ART OF SEWING
THE OLD WEST
THE EMERGENCE OF MAN
THE AMERICAN WILDERNESS
THE TIME-LIFE ENCYCLOPEDIA OF GARDENING
LIFE LIBRARY OF PHOTOGRAPHY
THIS FABULOUS CENTURY
FOODS OF THE WORLD
TIME-LIFE LIBRARY OF AMERICA
TIME-LIFE LIBRARY OF ART
GREAT AGES OF MAN
LIFE SCIENCE LIBRARY
THE LIFE HISTORY OF THE UNITED STATES
TIME READING PROGRAM
LIFE NATURE LIBRARY
LIFE WORLD LIBRARY
FAMILY LIBRARY:
  HOW THINGS WORK IN YOUR HOME
  THE TIME-LIFE BOOK OF THE FAMILY CAR
  THE TIME-LIFE FAMILY LEGAL GUIDE
  THE TIME-LIFE BOOK OF FAMILY FINANCE

*This volume is one of a series
that celebrates the history of
maritime adventure, from the Greek
trireme to the modern ocean liner.*

The Cover: Running before an offshore
wind under full sail, a Viking ship of the
Ninth Century courses gracefully over
the waves with its fierce dragon head
glowering out to sea in this re-creation
by artist Ken Townsend. Even with their
simple rigging and a single square sail,
Viking ships were able to hold a respectable
windward course, as the ship in the
background is doing while it skirts a coastal
mist preparing to tack for open waters.

The Title Page: Showing a masterful
sense of balance and textural contrasts, this
Ninth Century dragon head, 22 inches
long, reflects the high degree of artistry
attained by Viking craftsmen. It was
found on a Viking burial ship unearthed in
Oseberg, Norway, in 1904, and was used
as a talisman in religious ceremonies.

The Seafarers

THE VIKINGS

by Robert Wernick
AND THE EDITORS OF TIME-LIFE BOOKS

TIME-LIFE BOOKS, ALEXANDRIA, VIRGINIA

Time-Life Books Inc.
is a wholly owned subsidiary of
TIME INCORPORATED

FOUNDER: Henry R. Luce 1898-1967

Editor-in-Chief: Henry Anatole Grunwald
President: J. Richard Munro
Chairman of the Board: Ralph P. Davidson
Executive Vice President: Clifford J. Grum
Chairman, Executive Committee: James R. Shepley
Editorial Director: Ralph Graves
Group Vice President, Books: Joan D. Manley
Vice Chairman: Arthur Temple

TIME-LIFE BOOKS INC.

MANAGING EDITOR: Jerry Korn
Text Director: George Constable
Board of Editors: Dale M. Brown, George G. Daniels,
Thomas H. Flaherty Jr., Martin Mann, Philip W. Payne,
Gerry Schremp, Gerald Simons
Planning Director: Edward Brash
Art Director: Tom Suzuki
    Assistant: Arnold C. Holeywell
Director of Administration: David L. Harrison
Director of Operations: Gennaro C. Esposito
Director of Research: Carolyn L. Sackett
    Assistant: Phyllis K. Wise
Director of Photography: Dolores A. Littles

CHAIRMAN: John D. McSweeney
President: Carl G. Jaeger
Executive Vice Presidents: John Steven Maxwell,
David J. Walsh
Vice Presidents: George Artandi, Stephen L. Bair,
Peter G. Barnes, Nicholas Benton, John L. Canova,
Beatrice T. Dobie, Carol Flaumenhaft, James L. Mercer,
Herbert Sorkin, Paul R. Stewart

The Seafarers

Editor: George G. Daniels
Editorial Staff for The Vikings:
Picture Editor: Jane N. Coughran
Designer: Herbert H. Quarmby
Text Editors: Anne Horan, Sterling Seagrave
Staff Writers: William C. Banks, Carol Dana,
Stuart Gannes, Gus Hedberg
Chief Researcher: Charlotte A. Quinn
Researchers: Peggy L. Sawyer, Mary G. Burns,
Philip Brandt George, W. Mark Hamilton, Barbara Levitt,
Trudy W. Pearson, Blaine McCornick Reilly
Copy Coordinator: Sheirazada Hann
Art Assistant: Michelle René Clay
Picture Coordinator: Marguerite Johnson
Editorial Assistant: Adrienne George

Special Contributors
Champ Clark, David Thompson (text); Barbara Hicks,
Katie Hooper McGregor (research)

Editorial Operations
Production Director: Feliciano Madrid
    Assistants: Peter A. Inchauteguiz, Karen A. Meyerson
Copy Processing: Gordon E. Buck
Quality Control Director: Robert L. Young
    Assistant: James J. Cox
    Associates: Daniel J. McSweeney,
    Michael G. Wight
Art Coordinator: Anne B. Landry
Copy Room Director: Susan B. Galloway
    Assistants: Celia Beattie, Ricki Tarlow

Correspondents: Elisabeth Kraemer (Bonn); Margot
Hapgood, Dorothy Bacon (London); Susan Jonas, Lucy T.
Voulgaris (New York); Maria Vincenza Aloisi, Josephine
du Brusle (Paris); Ann Natanson (Rome).
Valuable assistance was also provided by: Mirka
Gondicas (Athens); Karin Hills, Ole Schierbeck
(Copenhagen); Robert Kroon (Geneva); Judy Aspinall,
Diana Brown, Penny Newman (London); Bill Lyon
(Madrid); Bruce W. Nelan, Felix Rosenthal (Moscow);
Carolyn T. Chubet, Miriam Hsia (New York); Dag
Christensen, Paul Jorgensen (Oslo); Bogi Agustsson,
Eidur Gudnason (Reykjavik); Mary Johnson (Stockholm);
Traudl Lessing (Vienna).

The Author:
Robert Wernick, a freelance writer living
in Paris, traveled extensively in areas once
ruled by the Vikings, gathering material in
Iceland, England, Normandy and throughout Scandinavia. A former staff member of
Life, he is the author of several Time-Life
Books, including The Monument Builders
in The Emergence of Man series.

The Consultants:
John Horace Parry, Gardiner Professor of
Oceanic History and Affairs at Harvard
University, took his Ph.D. at Cambridge
University. Among Parry's numerous his-
torical studies are The Discovery of the Sea
and The Spanish Seaborne Empire.

Richard N. Ringler, formerly Chairman of
the Department of Scandinavian Studies at
the University of Wisconsin, earned his
Ph.D. from Harvard. A specialist in medieval Scandinavian literature and culture,
he studied for a year at the University of
Iceland in Reykjavík, and traveled to the
Orkneys, Shetlands and Hebrides to study
the early Viking westward expansion.

Helge Braathen received his master's degree in Scandinavian archeology from the
University of Oslo, and is curator of the Ar-
keologisk Museum in Stavanger, Norway.
A scholar of political and social structures
of the Viking age, he is also an authority on
their burial customs, having studied ancient grave sites throughout Norway.

Birgitta Wallace, a staff archeologist for
the Canadian national park service, earned
her master's degree at the University of
Uppsala, Sweden, and later continued her
studies of the Viking age as a research associate at the Pittsburgh's Carnegie Museum. She supervises excavations at L'Anse
aux Meadows, Newfoundland, the only established Norse site in North America.

For information about any Time-Life book, please write:
Reader Information
Time-Life Books
541 North Fairbanks Court, Chicago, Illinois 60611

TIME-LIFE is a trademark of Time Incorporated U.S.A.

Library of Congress Cataloguing in Publication Data
Wernick, Robert (date)
    The vikings.
    (The seafarers; v.7)
    Bibliography: p.
    Includes index.
    1. Vikings.   2. Europe—History—476-1492.
I. Time-Life Books.   II. Title.   III. Series
DL65.W43   940.1   78-24119
ISBN 0-8094-2709-5
ISBN 0-8094-2708-7 lib. bdg.
ISBN 0-8094-2707-9 retail ed.

Contents

A conquering host rising out of the sea mists

"Is there any living man, king or prince, on land or water as bold as we? No one dares to meet us sword with sword. Be we right or wrong, all yield before us, plowman and merchant, horseman and ship."

So boasted a Viking chieftain in the year 866 as he set sail with a mighty host of 1,000 warriors to mount a major attack on England. He was a Dane, whose name comes down through history as Ivar the Boneless, presumably because he was double-jointed. He was, in any case, not a man given to idle boasts. At the time, much of Europe cowered before these marauding seafarers who swooped down from the North in their splendid ships.

The first Viking raids, commencing about 80 years earlier, had been hit-and-run affairs. A few shiploads of these huge and brawny men would suddenly appear out of the sea mists. They would pillage at will, mercilessly cutting down all opposition, then disappear over the waters as swiftly as they had come. But Ivar the Boneless had higher ambitions: he meant to conquer England and make that fertile, well-watered land his own.

Ivar embarked with his men and their arms in a fleet of dragon-prowed ships of war and sailed for three days across the North Sea. When he made his landfall on the coast of Kent, the overawed inhabitants desperately tried to buy peace from the Vikings. "And the people of Kent promised them money for that peace," related the historians of the day in the Anglo-Saxon Chronicle. "And under cover of the peace and promise of money, the Viking army stole away inland by night and ravaged all eastern Kent, for they knew that they would seize more money by secret plunder than by peace."

The Vikings next marched northward to attack the Northumbrian kingdom of York, a realm then torn by civil war. Too late York's squabbling rival kings decided to join forces to repel the Norsemen. "An immense slaughter was made of the Northumbrians, and both kings were killed," lamented the Chronicle.

After rampaging through central England, the Viking host wintered at Nottingham before returning in the spring of 868 to East Anglia. Here Ivar and his men defeated, horribly tortured and eventually killed yet another king, the beloved and devoutly Christian Edmund of East Anglia, who was later canonized by the Catholic Church for his noble fight against the heathen.

The Viking tide was finally stemmed by King Ethelred of Wessex and his brother Alfred—later to be called Alfred the Great. But it was not stemmed until the invaders had conquered more than half of all England, subjugated its citizens and parceled out the land themselves.

In the great age of the Vikings, between the 8th and the 11th Centuries, conquests such as that of Ivar the Boneless were repeated time and time again. Erupting out of Scandinavia, the water-borne warriors of Denmark, Norway and Sweden conquered much of the British Isles. They pillaged the coast of France, pushed inland to sack Paris and drove the Frankish overlords from Normandy. Sweeping south down the great rivers of central Europe, they overwhelmed the Slavs of Russia, seized Kiev and clashed with the Greeks at the very threshold of Constantinople, the great capital of the Byzantine Empire.

In all this the Vikings gained immense booty. But they were far more than latter-day barbarians, content merely to plunder and burn. As shrewd and intelligent as they were brave and brawny, they were builders of cities and founders of states, writers of poetry and givers of laws. The Vikings were supreme traders as well, and bold and tenacious explorers who ventured across distant oceans. Indeed, not since the golden age of the Roman Empire had any people so powerfully stamped the Western world with their personality and purpose.

Manning the oars of their double-ended craft, the fierce and powerfully armed Norsemen, led by Ivar, cross the North Sea to England in the year 866. Already, two ships have reached shore and the Vikings scurry across long gangplanks to an England represented at left as a wooded and heavily fortified island. In the following illuminations from an 11th Century English religious history, the Vikings are both a fearful and an elegant presence, vilified more by their actions than by their appearance, which is not unlike that of the peoples they came to conquer.

8

Seeking to escape the Vikings, a monk guides his cargo of precious relics across a rickety bridge under the hand of God. Rich monasteries and churches were a favorite Viking target, and clerics often had to choose between flight and martyrdom.

Towering over his troops, Ivar outlines his demands for surrender to a messenger (center right), who will convey them to King Edmund of East Anglia. A typical Viking, Ivar sought a bargain that would bring the plunder of victory without fighting.

Disarmed but still wearing his crown and robes, the pious Edmund—defeated by the Danes in 869 after refusing to surrender to Ivar—is dragged from his church in Hoxne. At right, his hand on his sword, a Danish chieftain orders Edmund to his doom.

After binding the hapless King Edmund to an oak tree, Viking archers let fly their arrows, piercing the defeated English monarch with their shafts until he resembled, as a church chronicler later wrote, a sea "urchin whose skin is closely set with quills."

Viking pikemen scale the ramparts of the ill-defended town
of Thetford in East Anglia while their sword-wielding comrades
below break through an archway and begin to slaughter the
town's inhabitants, who cringe and plead screaming for mercy.

While oarsmen steady their vessels, soldiers of the Viking army
board longships in 880, departing English soil after 15 years
to fight on the Continent, where, wrote a contemporary chronicler,
they "raged savagely in nearly every kingdom of the Franks."

"From the fury of the Northmen deliver us, O Lord"

hey came out of the cold and hostile north on a June day in 793 A.D.—long, low, black ships with tall, curving prows and broad, red-and-white sails, dancing over the waves toward the English island of Lindisfarne off the coast of Northumbria. The ships plunged straight onto the beach, and out poured a band of huge, shaggy men, howling like animals and waving swords. In an instant they swarmed up the island's grassy slopes, where herds of fat sheep and cattle grazed peacefully in the meadows, ready for slaughtering.

But Lindisfarne had far greater attractions for the invaders than fresh provisions. On the island stood a venerable Christian monastery to which generations of the pious and the wicked had bequeathed riches for the repose of their souls. In its chapels and on its altars lay a profusion of golden crucifixes, silver pyxes and ciboria; ivory reliquaries; precious tapestries woven of silk and linen; and books of illuminated vellum encrusted with precious stones.

To the monks surrounded by these riches, the monastery at Lindisfarne was more than a repository of worldly wealth; it was a center of learning and a sanctuary for contemplation. The monks spent their days praying, chanting orisons, inscribing manuscripts, corresponding with fellow monks throughout Christendom and chronicling the events of their times. On the entire island there was not a single armed man, and it was unthinkable that any God-fearing soul would dare lay unlawful hands on the monks' property.

The intruders from the sea had no reverence for the Christian God, no scruples about plundering a Christian sanctuary and scant regard for human life. They fell with their swords upon the monks. Some of the brothers were cut down and killed in front of their altars; some were thrown into the sea to drown, and some were stripped naked and driven out of the monastery to the hoots and jeers of the invaders. The sacred buildings were denuded of their gold and silver, illuminated manuscripts and jewels, and the treasure was carried down to the beach. There the raiders loaded their waiting ships. Long before an alarm could be sent out, these vessels, now heavy with booty, had vanished over the dark gray waters of the North Sea whence they had come.

This was an atrocity unprecedented in the memory of living man, and the terrible news flew as fast as messengers on foot, on horseback and on shipboard could take it throughout the scattered Anglo-Saxon kingdoms and beyond.

Before long, the news had crossed the English Channel to the land of the Franks, where Alcuin, another Anglo-Saxon monk and ranking scholar of the age, was supervising a renaissance of learning at the court

Brandishing swords and axes, Vikings march relentlessly across a priory stone, carved to commemorate the 793 raid on the Lindisfarne monastery. Ushering in 300 years of depredations, this bloody incident, according to the Ninth Century Anglo-Saxon Chronicle, was presaged by such terrible omens as "whirlwinds and flashes of lightning, and fiery dragons flying in the air."

of the Emperor Charlemagne at Aachen. Alcuin, expressing the shock and dismay of his fellow believers throughout Christendom, wrote, "It is nearly 350 years that we and our fathers have inhabited in this most lovely land, and never before has such a terror appeared in Britain as this that we have just suffered from a pagan race." To Alcuin and his contemporaries, the desecration of the monastery was not only appalling; it was astounding, in a day when sailors were not known to venture out of sight of land, "that such an inroad from the sea could be made."

Alcuin little guessed at the terrors yet to rise out of the sea in his lifetime, and for many lifetimes to come—terrors that would make Lindisfarne seem no more than a minor act of vandalism. The pagan people to whom he referred were the Norsemen, with whom British and European merchants already had a nodding acquaintance as traders. Soon these raiders would be known throughout Christendom as the Vikings, and viewed as a scourge to the civilized world. Many, like Alcuin, saw in the Vikings' riot of death and destruction a fulfillment of the words of the Old Testament Prophet Jeremiah—"out of the north evil shall break forth upon all the inhabitants of the land"—and thought the Day of Judgment might well be at hand.

The summer after the raid on Lindisfarne, the Vikings descended upon Jarrow, about 50 miles down the Northumbrian coast, and struck a blow at the monastery that once was the residence of the Venerable Bede, perhaps the greatest historian, theologian and astronomer of his time. In the summer of 795 the Vikings ravaged Iona, off the coast of Scotland, and Morganwg on the southern coast of Wales. In 797 it was the turn of the Isle of Man, and in 800 of a monastery just south of Jarrow, and another, more distant, on the west coast of Scotland. Before long, it was said, the monastery chapels and village churches of England rang with a new prayer: *A furore Normannorum libera nos, Domine*—"From the fury of the Northmen deliver us, O Lord."

And still the Northmen came. Those swift hit-and-run summertime raids at the close of the Eighth Century were just preliminary stirrings of what was to become an epic movement lasting nearly 300 years. From about 800 onward, the Vikings swept south, west and east as if borne on a tidal wave—swelling in numbers and spilling farther and farther afield. "The wild beasts," wrote the French monk Abbo, "go through hills and fields, killing babies, children, young men, old men, fathers, sons and mothers. They overthrow, they destroy, they ravage; sinister cohort, fatal phalanx, cruel host."

Sometimes the Vikings struck the same places again and again. The great Irish monastery of Armagh, chosen by St. Patrick as the seat of his church in the early Fifth Century, was to be plundered five times—three of them in one month in 832. The port of Dorestad on the Rhine, the biggest commercial center of northern Europe, was robbed, wasted, depopulated at least six times, according to one chronicler. No one knew where the Viking raiders would strike, or when, or in what numbers; Hamburg was sacked, Paris was burned. As fear and foreboding overcame the settled people of Europe, "it seemed," wrote one monk, "that all Christian people would perish."

Wulfstan, an 11th Century Anglo-Saxon archbishop, puts quill to page in this illustration from an early manuscript. Wulfstan and other Christian chroniclers provided most of the few contemporary accounts of Viking raids, filling the annals of the Church with descriptions of bloodstained altars and trampled relics. They interpreted the raids as divine vengeance for human sins, and employed their lurid litanies to startle their countrymen into renewed spiritual—and material—commitments to the Church.

The Irish author of a dire 12th Century volume entitled *The War of the Irish with the Foreigners* spoke for all Europe when he cried out from the depths of rage and misery: "Although there were a hundred hard, steeled iron heads on one neck and a hundred sharp, ready, cool, never-rusting, brazen tongues in each head and a hundred garrulous, loud, unceasing voices from each tongue, they could not recount, or narrate, or enumerate, or tell what all the Irish suffered in common, both men and women, laity and clergy, old and young, noble and ignoble, of hardship and of injury and of oppression in every house, from these valiant, wrathful, purely pagan people."

Such was the portrait of the Vikings drawn by monks. Yet Vikings had another side, one that anxious monks could not see or appreciate—an enormously constructive and creative side. And in the long run this was far more important than all the fire and fury of their raids and incursions.

The Norsemen may have begun as raiders, but they developed into skilled conquerors and efficient administrators. They established long-lived states at the ends of Europe, east and west and south. They taught the wild Slavic inhabitants of what is now Russia the rudiments of civil government. The duchy of Normandy in northern France was a Viking creation that by the standards of the time was a model state, with a more tightly centralized government than anything the West had seen since the overthrow of Rome centuries before.

The Vikings were brilliant tradesmen as well, canny, enterprising, risk-taking merchants, always on the lookout for new routes of commerce to open, or old ones to revive. They brought fresh goods and fresh ideas into the society of the West and played a decisive role in spawning the new breed of feudal lords that would arise in the Middle Ages.

Though they came from an almost wholly rural society—with no more than a few towns in all their land—they became town builders when the occasion demanded. Plundering the backward agricultural-pastoral kingdoms of Ireland, they found it profitable to build a chain of market towns all around the coasts that became cities and provided the Irish for the first time with the stimulus and challenge of urban life.

The Vikings were foot-loose and adventurous and brave as lions, all qualities that fitted them admirably to serve as mercenary soldiers for foreign rulers. When the ruler was brave himself, and generous, they fought for him to the death. Vikings formed the private bodyguard of the Roman emperors of Byzantium and helped their doomed but dazzling realm to survive for another half millennium.

All this the Vikings could accomplish because they were the most mobile people of their age, masters of those greatest of highroads, the seas and rivers and lakes. The Viking genius was born of the water; they were never more at home than when scudding along distant courses in the ships they had built with vast thought and craftsmen's care, the fastest and finest vessels the world had ever known.

At their most daring, they took these superb ships out across the western oceans into waters where, so far as they knew, no man had ever before sailed. And when they found empty lands in the northern waters, they turned into tenacious colonists. In desolate Iceland they built the

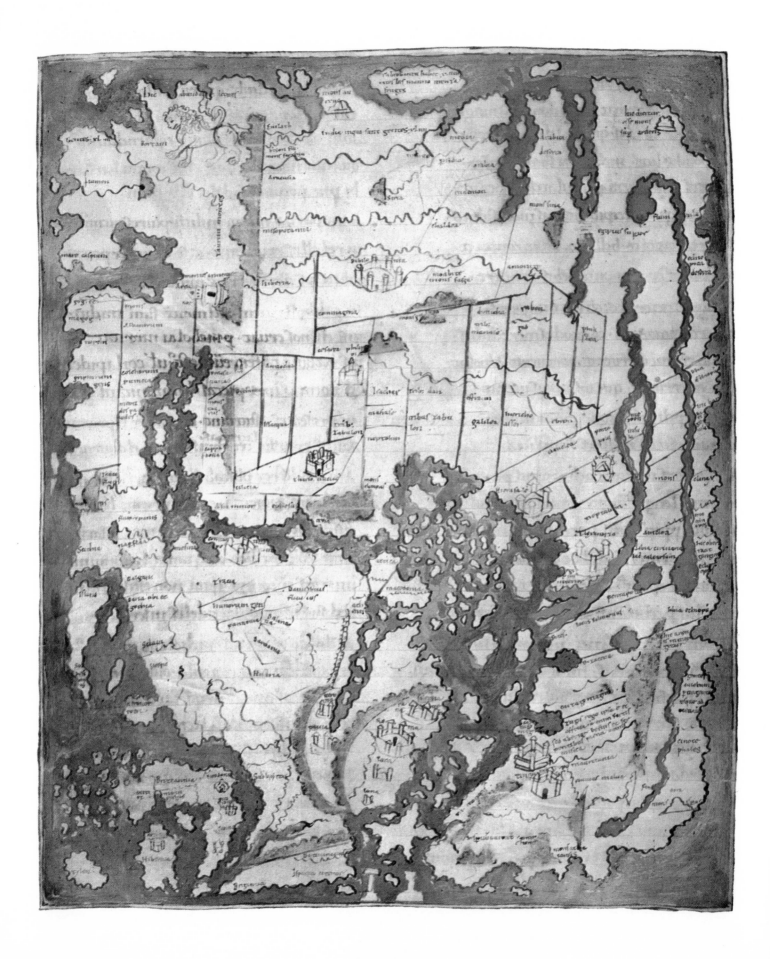

first republic of modern Europe, and then they ventured far beyond to become the first Europeans to set foot on the great ice-capped mass of Greenland and on the more inviting shores of North America.

Much about these lusty, feisty, inquisitive, wide-ranging adventurers remains a mystery—including the very name by which they are known. No one is sure where the word Viking came from or what it originally meant. Various etymologists have traced it to various Old Norse words, from *vik*, meaning "inlet," because the Vikings' Scandinavian homeland was riven by fjords; from *vig*, meaning "battle," because they were so skilled in making wars, and from *vikja*, meaning "to turn aside, to deviate"—a comment on their wiles and wanderings.

Whatever its origin, the word quickly acquired, for the peoples of Europe, a meaning it has never lost: a seaborne rover, raider, conqueror, full of courage, guile and brute strength. It meant much the same to the Vikings themselves. When a Norseman said he was going a-Viking, as bold and ambitious men in the Scandinavian lands dreamed of doing throughout the 9th and 10th Centuries, he meant that he would outfit a ship to sail over the high seas in search of plunder and adventure. Both of these—as far as the Vikings were concerned—were eminently respectable goals. Yet there was always an ambiguity about the term; Vikings were just as likely, for one reason or another, to turn their prows against their own neighbors as against distant foreigners. And when they did, those who had been harmed would scour the seas to punish them. Once a band of Vikings settled down and made a territory their own, they did not like being preyed upon any better than anyone else—as witness Earl Magnus, a Viking born in the Orkney Islands, who was commended in a saga as being "severe and unsparing" toward robbers and sea raiders.

The origin of the name Viking is only the first of the puzzles associated with the Norsemen. Virtually everything that is known about them comes from obscure and incomplete ancient sources, and from modern archeology, which has only begun to piece together the history of this fascinating people.

The most nearly contemporaneous of the written sources are the manuscripts of the clerics, such as those of Alcuin, Abbo and Adam of Bremen. Their writings, combined with secular histories like the Anglo-Saxon and Russian chronicles, present hundreds of firsthand commentaries and reports. But at the same time, these records are likely to be biased, since they were written by the victims of the Vikings' depredations or by partisans of the victims. Other written accounts were left by acquaintances of the Vikings, such as the Arab merchants who encountered them in the marketplaces around Scandinavia and Continental Europe. But these proud Muslims were not much more favorably disposed toward the Vikings than were the Christian monks; coming from an infinitely more settled civilization, they looked upon the Vikings as crude and uncouth. "They are the filthiest of God's creatures," wrote the Arab traveler Ibn Fadlan. "They do not wash after discharging their natural functions; neither do they wash their hands after meals. They are as stray donkeys."

The Vikings themselves, alas, kept neither logs at sea nor annals ashore. Until the 11th Century, they wrote scarcely anything save runic inscriptions on grave and crossroad markers (pages 106-107). The only surviving accounts in their own tongue are the sagas—the legends of their heroic age, which were transmitted orally from generation to generation and not written down till long after the Viking age had ended.

The sagas are, however, a treasure-trove of information. They tell much about how the Vikings lived, loved, worshipped, waged war, hunted, traded, explored. And the picturesque names by which they knew their epic figures conjure up much about their character and their behavior: King Eric Bloodaxe and Thorfinn Skullsplitter, known for their prowess in battle; Onund Treefoot, who had a leg cut off in a sea fight and stumped around on a wooden one thereafter; Olaf Peacock, who loved fine clothes; and Sigurd Sow, who, though he was a king, dressed in old clothes and was always rooting around in his fields like an ordinary dirt farmer.

As might be expected with histories committed to paper centuries after the fact, the sagas are riddled with contradictions, ambiguities and mystifying obscurities. The authors often tended to be maddeningly brief and matter-of-fact about the most dramatic of happenings. Nevertheless, for all their shortcomings, the sagas remain the truest measure for reckoning the values the Vikings lived by and for viewing their heroes and villains through their own eyes. Moreover, archeology has confirmed some of what the sagas recount—as it has the events recorded in the Christian chronicles.

At the dawn of the Ninth Century, when they began their raids on coastal Britain, the Vikings who erupted out of Scandinavia were essentially a single people then barely on the threshold of dividing into the three nations of Norway, Sweden and Denmark. They spoke the same language, Old Norse. They lived the same rugged life on isolated farmsteads, usually near a body of water. They worshipped the same gods, and their bards sang the same songs to honor the same warrior ancestors.

They were descended directly from the Germanic tribes that fanned out over Continental Europe between the First and Fifth Centuries A.D. and brought down the Roman Empire. But earlier ancestors of the Norsemen can be traced much further back, to 6000 B.C. By that date, men and women were paddling in primitive craft among Denmark's 600 islands, into the deep and narrow fjords that cut from the sea through Norway's craggy mountains and over the thousands of lakes and rivers that lace Sweden. The people who used these craft were nomads moving from one hunting ground to another; presumably they paddled offshore in pursuit of seal, porpoise and whale.

Two millennia later these nomads were joined by a new wave of migrants and settled down to plant farms and live in permanent dwellings—but still the boat provided their major form of food, which was fish. By 1500 B.C. they had loaded their craft with flint tools and Baltic amber—some of it worked into jewelry, some of it raw—and were venturing as far as Ireland and Britain to barter for gold, copper and tin. No oceangoing vessels of that era have been found, but the goods, unquestionably Scandinavian, have been uncovered in the British Isles.

Horns for worship not war

According to popular legend, Viking warriors went into battle wearing huge horned helmets that struck terror into the hearts of their opponents. In fact, warriors never wore such headgear in combat.

Dating from the Bronze Age in Scandinavia, between 1800 B.C. and 500 B.C., these helmets were restricted to the wealthy and noble, and were used for ceremony: to celebrate the initiation of young men into the brotherhood of warriors, and to worship deities. When they actually dressed for battle, the Vikings donned simple conical caps of iron or leather—if they deigned to wear any protection at all.

Wearing a horned helmet, this four-inch kneeling figure of a Bronze Age deity comes from the Danish island of Zealand.

Paradoxically, the very seas and fjords that from time immemorial inspired the Scandinavians to build boats—thus making possible both travel and communication—simultaneously bred in them traits of separateness and regional pride. Living in isolated pockets of land—where they wrested a living from an ungenerous earth that was rock-strewn and frequently frost-bound—they developed proud independence and fierce loyalties to their communities.

A Viking farmstead raised crops of oats, barley, rye and cabbage to supplement the haul from the sea, and it raised flocks of geese and herds of cattle, goats, sheep and pigs to provide both food and raw materials (horn, skin, feathers and wool) for tools, for clothing and for the boat that was certain to be among its goods and chattels. On the farmstead stood a large building that housed perhaps as many as a dozen people, including two or three slaves who labored as farm hands and general helpers. The house might be faced with timber, stone, sod, or wattle and daub, depending on what materials were at hand.

Indoors, benches lined the walls of the central hall. The center seat was often raised to form a sort of throne of honor, and it was flanked by two pillars that were more symbolic than functional. The sagas related that all of the indoor woodwork, and especially the high-seat pillars, was heavily carved, frequently with geometric and floral designs and occasionally with representations of a deity such as the ever-popular Thor. In such a hall, presiding in his high seat and surrounded by his sons and followers, sat the *bondi*, the proprietor of the farm, a self-reliant, self-sufficient patriarch.

A Viking community might have a cluster of such houses huddled together, village fashion, or it might have several scattered over a valley that reached from the waterside to a mountain boundary. In either case the community was generally populated by a family, or several families, who were related down to third cousins, even fourth cousins—people who shared a common great-great-great-grandfather.

These extended families formed federations with other extended families that occupied neighboring territories. Such federations shared enterprises of hunting and fishing, defense and trade—and, as the practice grew after the end of the Eighth Century, raiding into foreign lands. Each extended family had its chieftain, known as a *jarl*, or "earl," and in times of stress natural leaders emerged from among the chieftains. Here and there such a leader might be known as a *konungr*—Old Norse meaning literally "man of noted origin," and related to the English word king.

In the early Viking days such a petty king was by no means a national monarch; he was merely the leading figure in his region, large or small. Norway, Denmark and Sweden began to emerge only after the strongest of these petty kings had subdued and unified a number of lesser kings and jarls, often after long and bloody fighting. Not until the middle 870s—some 80 years after the raid on Lindisfarne—did Norway acquire a king, in the person of Harald Fairhair; Denmark and Sweden lagged more than 100 years behind Norway, with Svein Forkbeard ascending in Denmark in 985 and Olaf Skautkonung coming to rule Sweden in 993. Even then the boundaries of the three nations continued to shift far beyond the Middle Ages, and the position of the kings themselves de-

Varied portraits of many-sided men

His mouth wide with menace, a Viking warrior roars at his enemies in this Ninth Century Norwegian wood carving. Decorating a cart found in a burial mound, the face may have been carved to express the Viking ferocity and thus keep away marauding spirits of the hereafter.

Wherever the Vikings set foot, they immediately and perforce became objects of an intense and abiding interest among friend and foe alike. The historical accounts of medieval Europe and Asia Minor abound in descriptions of these huge, tangle-haired men, so "utterly wild and rough," wrote one awed chronicler in Russia, that "they evidence their bloodthirstiness by their very appearance."

An Arab trader who encountered the Vikings in western Russia described them as men "with vast frames and great courage"; they "know not defeat." Another contemporary chronicler recalled that in battle they moved their bodies like "hurricanes or typhoons or floods." Adam of Bremen noted that "they use the pelts of wild beasts for clothing and in speaking to one another gnash their teeth rather than utter words."

The Viking in art was no less fascinating a subject. His portrait decorated historical and religious chronicles and church interiors and was hewn out of wood, woven in tapestries, even whittled out of walrus tusks. In their own views of themselves, Vikings often exhibited visages of nightmarish ferocity, for the Vikings enjoyed thinking of themselves as fear-inspiring warriors.

A sword and shield are always ready for a hooded warrior in this 11th Century Byzantine mosaic. The Vikings were favored recruits for the Varangian Guard, the elite military corps of the Byzantine Empire, cutting handsome figures in their uniforms. Relates one saga, "Womenfolk paid no heed to anything but to gaze at all their finery."

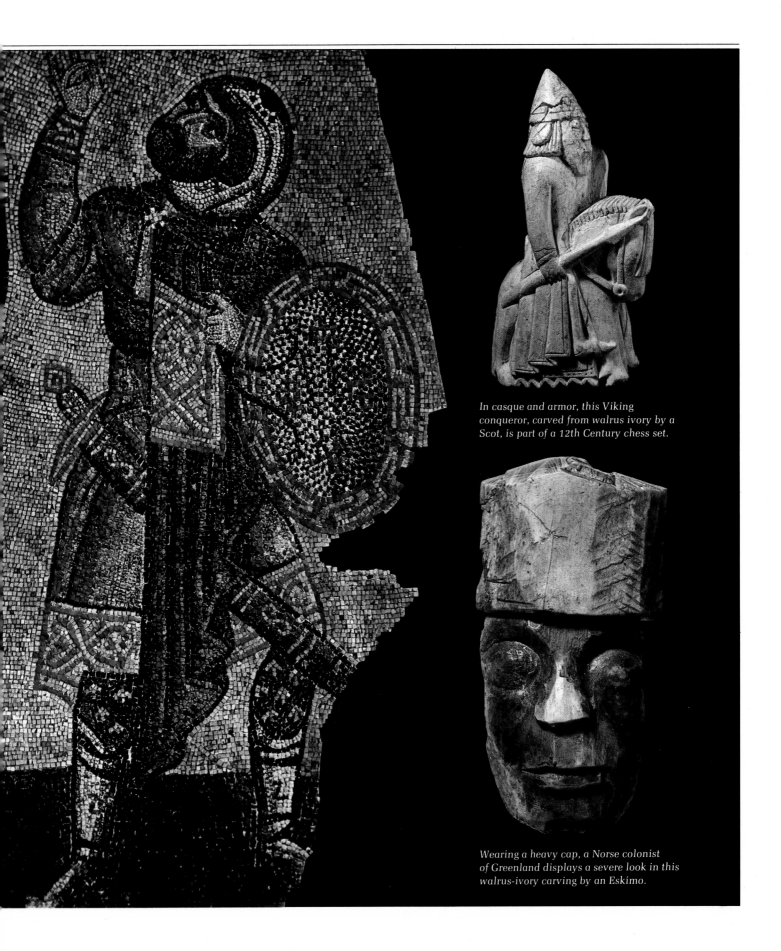

In casque and armor, this Viking conqueror, carved from walrus ivory by a Scot, is part of a 12th Century chess set.

Wearing a heavy cap, a Norse colonist of Greenland displays a severe look in this walrus-ivory carving by an Eskimo.

pended upon the acceptance of their people—or their own strength and skill in forcing that acceptance.

A Viking leader, whether a king leading an invasion or a jarl instigating a local brawl with another chieftain, was expected to be in the forefront of the fight and to perform feats of strength beyond the capacities of other men. Bloodthirsty, greathearted Olaf Tryggvason, who ruled a part of Norway at the close of the 10th Century, was one of the most admired of Viking kings, not least because, as the saga devoted to his life says, he could hurl two spears at once, one with each hand, and because he could leap over the gunwale of his great dragon-prowed ship and bound from oar to oar while his men were rowing.

It was a rare occurrence in the early days for a ruler to succeed in passing his crown to a son unless that son was prepared to fight fiercely for the right to retain it. The Vikings had no long-established closed aristocracy. The bondis who made up the bulk of the population recognized only force of will and arms, and as free men and warriors as well as farmers, no doubt many among them nurtured ambitions of becoming jarls or even kings.

The dominant preoccupation in a bondi's life was family. His first loyalty was to his relatives; his prime ambition was to increase the fortune and fame of his family; his first duty was to defend its honor against the greed and affronts of others. That honor might be challenged any time a quarrel broke out, over any pretext: the size of a dowry, the theft of a sheep, the rights to a stranded whale. Such a challenge demanded satisfaction; thus blood feuds were part of the normal pattern of the Norseman's life.

At any moment, relate the sagas, the daily round of farming, herding, fishing, might be torn asunder; a single spark of violence might set off an endless round of duels, ambushes, pitched battles, killings, maimings and burnings. These blood feuds were pursued with malignant intensity, as each fresh killing stoked the furnace of hate. "I would ask this of you, that you forgive me for whatever I have done against you," said Thord Andreassson in a saga when he had fallen into the hands of his enemy, a jarl named Gizur. "That I will do," replied Gizur in the cold, dispassionate tone that had been his since the day his whole family had been massacred by Thord and his friends, "as soon as you are dead." Thord tried to break away but was felled by an ax stroke in the back of the neck delivered by one of Gizur's followers.

Anyone stood ready to help sustain a feud—even a king. Another saga tells how one day at the court of King Magnus the Good, Asmund Grankelsson, one of Magnus' men, looked down to the harbor and there saw his enemy, Harek of Thjotta, landing from his ship. "I will pay Harek for my father's murder," cried Asmund, brandishing his weapon, which was only a thin sort of hatchet. "Rather take this ax of mine," said the King to Asmund; "there are hard bones in the old fellow." And he gave him a thick one, with a handle like a club. Asmund took the King's ax without a word, went down and plunged it into Harek's skull with such ferocity that the ax edge was bent by the blow.

The Viking woman was bred to be mate to such a man. She had to be sturdy and self-reliant, for she might have to assume responsibility for

Wearing a conical battle helmet, Thor, Viking god of thunder, clutches his mighty hammer with both hands in this 10th Century Icelandic statuette. Three inches tall and cast in bronze, the figure was probably a good-luck talisman, and the emphatic crosslike design of the hammer leads experts to suggest that the Viking craftsman may also have been seeking the additional blessing of Christianity, a religion beginning to gain favor in Iceland at the time.

family and farm while her husband was away fighting or seafaring. And she was a stickler for family honor—understandably, for there was scarcely a Viking woman who had not seen a father or brother or husband carried home broken and bloody from a fight. Unlike the men, she did not bear arms and could not take out her grief and rage in physical violence. But she could—and did—insist that the menfolk return her an eye for an eye, a tooth for a tooth.

A saga recounts how an Icelandic chieftain named Flosi made a rare effort to stop the killings between his family and that of a neighbor named Njal. Flosi had been willing to accept a payment of money in atonement for the murder of his niece's husband, Hoskuld. But his move to pacify the quarrel got him nowhere. His widowed niece, Hildigunn, taunted him with being a coward and threw at him the awful, blood-clotted shirt in which her husband had been slain. She goaded Flosi into slaughtering Njal and all his sons; the act in turn led Njal's son-in-law to take threefold vengeance on Flosi and his family and friends. There seemed to be no way to end such feuds; they went on and on in perpetuity—or until one clan was utterly wiped out.

The sagas make so much of the incessant feuding and bloodletting that it is a wonder the Vikings had any energies left to work their farms—to say nothing of joining forces to raid abroad. Possibly the ancient storytellers gave an exaggerated idea of the extent of the feuds, though they were surely a large factor in Viking life.

In any case, death held no terrors for the Viking warrior. If he fought with valor, he could expect to be summoned by the god Odin to join his fellow heroes in the golden celestial realm of Asgard and live in the great hall of Valhalla, where a man could feast and fight forevermore. The Viking gods who presided over the heavenly and earthly arenas were lusty fellows, cast from the same rough mold as the Vikings themselves. Leading the pantheon was Odin, one-eyed magic god of wisdom, war and frenzy, a spirit of great cunning and bravery, protector of chieftains and poets alike. There was Thor, a stormy-tempered, hammer-wielding redhead who, as a slayer of giants and ruler of winds and rain, was a favorite among soldiers, seafarers and farmers. And there was Frey, a lascivious god of peace and fertility who helped to assure a bountiful harvest on land and sea. Frey possessed perhaps the most enviable of Viking equipment—a collapsible boat that could be folded up to fit into a small pouch when not in use and expanded to accommodate the entire company of the gods at Frey's command.

These Viking gods had won their treasures of silver and gold by conquest and theft, by feats of daring and guile—just as did the mortal Vikings. And as Viking gods stole like men, so did they rage and fight. In Scandinavian literature the Viking god Thor is the essence of the hard-drinking pugilistic Viking age. In one poem he devours an ox, eight salmon and three cups of mead at a single meal; in others he smashes enemy giants and demons by hurling boulders, thunderbolts and his boomerang-like hammer into their mighty skulls.

By the early Ninth Century some earnest Christian missionaries had begun to compete for heathen Viking souls by teaching them the Gospel.

Louis the Pious, the French king who reigned in France when the Vikings were beginning to settle there, periodically staged elaborate baptismal ceremonies to receive them into the Christian faith. The Vikings were willing enough to add yet another god to their pantheon, and many of them seem to have gone cheerfully through any number of Christian rituals for the prize to be had. On one occasion there were so many Christian converts that there was not enough cloth for the long white baptismal gowns that were customarily given out on such occasions. So the cloth was cut into smaller pieces to make it go further. The oldest of the Vikings was then heard to complain loudly that this was the 20th time he had been baptized, and he had always got a beautiful gown out of it, but this sack they had issued to him was "fit only for a cowherd, and if I were not ashamed of being naked, you could immediately give it back to your Christ."

In time, Christianity won some sincere followers among the Vikings—but even then the Norsemen took to the new faith with ambivalence. Of Helgi the Lean, son of a Swedish sea rover and an Irish princess, it was noted that "he believed in Christ and yet made vows to Thor for sea voyages and in tight corners and for everything that struck him as of real importance."

Even to his own gods—who remained powerful long after the rise of Christianity in Scandinavia—the Viking pledged his trust only on condition of mutual benefit. The saga of Hrafnkel illustrates how a Viking could rage when he felt betrayed by a god. Hrafnkel worshipped the god Frey. So solicitous was he of Frey that, when a harmless shepherd unwittingly made the mistake of riding a stallion that Hrafnkel had consecrated to the god, Hrafnkel killed the poor shepherd in cold blood. But then, against all expectations, the lowly shepherd's family succeeded in getting support from another rich landowner, who set out to avenge the slain shepherd. The landowner and the shepherd's kin caught Hrafnkel by surprise, stripped him of all his worldly possessions and cast him out into the bleak land.

At that point Hrafnkel angrily declared that he would no longer worship either Frey or the other gods if they could not take better care of him. Having decided to trust only to his wily, ruthless nature, he painfully won his way back to material prosperity—and then opened a new cycle of violence by seeking a bloody revenge on his foes.

The Vikings loved such tales of fortitude and independence in the face of adversity. They roared with approval upon hearing of the old bondi who boasted: "At one time the peace had lasted so long I was afraid I might come to die of old age, within doors upon a bed." And they liked to think of themselves in the image of such dashing figures as Gunnar Hamundarson, one of the heroes in the sagas, "a tall, powerful man" whose sword strokes "were so fast that he seemed to be brandishing three swords at once." Gunnar had looks as well as talents, with his "fair skin and a straight nose slightly tilted at the tip, keen blue eyes, red cheeks and fine head of thick flaxen hair."

Another popular figure was Skarphedin Njalsson, who one day caught sight of his hated foe Thrain Sigfusson standing with a troop of followers

The Vikings' belief in the afterlife and earthly demons is seen in two scenes from an Icelandic manuscript. The skyline is filled with the towers of Valhalla, whose 540 doorways allowed 800 warriors to enter side by side. At right, a giant serpent, thought to cause ocean tempests, snaps at an ox head dangled by Thor.

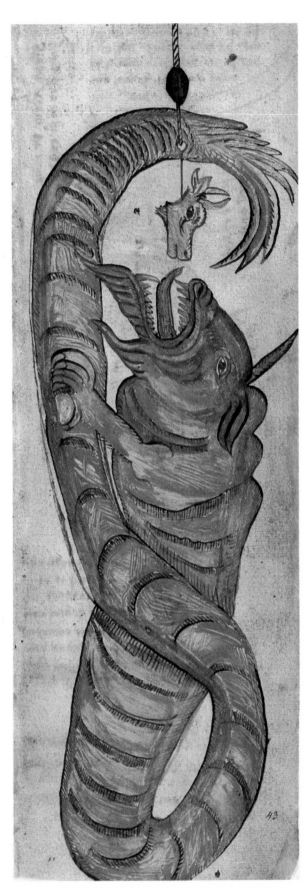

on an ice floe across a great gap of running water. Skarphedin made a prodigious leap over the water, holding his ax over his head, and came sliding along the ice so fast that Thrain was still putting on his helmet when down came the blow, clear to his jaw, "spilling the back teeth onto the ice." And leaping over a shield that was thrown in his way, Skarphedin slid on to safety before any of the crowd of his enemies could so much as strike a blow at him.

Honor and daring, valor, strength and agility, all these were qualities the Vikings prized and upheld. There was another, somewhat less admirable side to their nature as warriors that the Vikings were only too pleased to emphasize. This was their wild ferocity and brutality toward their foes. Indeed they seem to have exaggerated it deliberately in order to overawe their enemies. Just as they carved the prows of their ships in the shape of dragons and other horrid beasts to terrify the superstitious as they came surging out of the sea, so they cunningly circulated tales of their own savagery. One horrifying tale describes how, after a battle between Danish Vikings and two English kings in 867, the Norsemen broke open the rib cage of the captured King Ella of Northumbria and ripped his lungs out of his back—something they called carving the blood eagle, in allusion to the two lobes flapping like wings with the last dying breaths of the victim. Stories of such tortures, passed by Vikings and vanquished alike, conveyed the clear message to peoples everywhere that it would be wiser to yield than to try to thwart the relentless drive of the Norsemen.

Such cruelty was not the figment of a saga writer's imagination; it occurred all too often. So did another kind of wild behavior attributed to the Vikings, the bizarre actions with which some of them swarmed into battle. They would roll their eyes, bite the edge of their shields and utter animal howls. They would rush toward their adversaries without thought of pain or danger, sometimes without any protective armor. A warrior who behaved this way was called a *berserkr*, an Old Norse word that has variously been interpreted as "bare skin," meaning without shirt, and "bearskin," in possible reference to animal skins some of the men might have worn. Anglicized to "berserk," the word came to symbolize the Viking terror. Not every Viking fought that way, of course. Modern scholars suggest that such fantastic behavior may have been the result of drunken rages brought on by great drafts of ale or wine just before combat, or of paranoia or possibly of genetic flaws in individuals.

Whatever the cause, a number of Vikings—no one knows the percentage—did go berserk when they fought. And some kings and jarls found it useful to have bodyguards made up of these men, or to use them as shock troops or simply to spread terror wherever they went.

With fighting occupying so much of their thinking at home and abroad, it would seem that the Norsemen lived by no laws at all. But such was not the case. Viking laws, like Viking literature, evolved out of age-old traditions; they were committed to memory, transmitted orally and, when the occasion demanded, were recited aloud by a learned lawgiver.

Under Viking law, a jarl or a bondi charged with a crime such as theft or murder was brought before a court of judges made up of his peers. The accused could plead either guilty or innocent, and if the latter, he could go on to argue his case by calling witnesses to testify both to the facts and to his honesty and good character. To further substantiate his case, he could request—or the judges could demand—trial by ordeal.

Such an ordeal usually began on a Wednesday, the day of Odin, god of wisdom. The individual was given a handful of red-hot stones or scraps of metal to hold for a dreadful moment or two, and then sent away with a bandage until Saturday, when the judges reconvened to look him over and reach a consensus. Their decision was based not on whether his hand was burned, which it invariably was, but rather on the severity and the cleanliness of the burn. If it was clean, the defendant was deemed to be innocent; if it was festering, then he was pronounced guilty and given a punishment that ranged from a fine of money or merchandise to outlawry.

A man found guilty of wounding one of his peers in a brawl was required to make "bone payment" to the victim in silver coins—one eyrir for a small wound, six for a large one—and to pay for the cost of treatment. "If a wound needs cauterizing," the law said, then the same eyrir "is payable every time cauterizing is necessary. But as physician's fee, one eyrir is to be paid every month, and two months' worth of flour and two of butter. He who did the wounding must pay."

Another law decreed a series of fines for unseemly touching of a woman: four ounces of silver for touching her wrist or her ankle, two and two-thirds ounces for touching her elbow. But a touch above the knee, the law continued (whether with tongue in cheek or in dead earnest is not recorded) "is called the fool's clasp; no money is payable for that—most women put up with it when it goes that far."

There was certainly no humor to the other punishment to which miscreants might be condemned, and that was outlawry. A man found guilty of murder might be declared an outlaw, either for a limited period—a few months or a few years—or forever. As an outlaw, he could not fish, trade, join a Viking expedition or ask assistance in an hour of need—not even from a member of his family. Permanent outlawry was tantamount to banishment. Men on whom that lonely sentence fell had no recourse but to flee. Outlawry was in fact the reason that many a Viking left his homeland.

As in most early societies, right went hand in hand with might, and enforcement of the laws depended in large measure on who was strongest, complainant or defendant. A king or powerful jarl might seek to uphold the laws as a matter of self-interest in order to consolidate his rule. But where no such enforcement existed, a Viking might refuse to accept the judgment of a court or might decline to appear altogether. In that case the injured party—and his angered family—had no recourse but to seek restitution, if necessary in blood. And this was one of the primary reasons for the internecine fighting and bloodshed that raged throughout the Viking age.

The question remains, Why the sudden explosion of Viking energy at the end of the Eighth Century? Not the least extraordinary thing about the Viking achievement is that there were so few Vikings. Scandinavia was not thickly populated; no more than two million souls could have been living there when the Viking age opened at the dawn of the Ninth Century. That was only a small fraction of the population of the empire that Charlemagne bequeathed his son in 814.

One principal reason for expansion overseas was that the Scandinavian population, though small in absolute terms, was growing rapidly—too rapidly to be peacefully absorbed into Norse society. Medieval ecclesiastics of other lands, observing this sudden explosion of Vikings out of the North, ascribed it to the sexual prowess of the northern heathen. They were polygamous, said Adam of Bremen, and therefore had swarms of children. They had wild, promiscuous rites of spring every year, insisted the Norman chronicler Dudo of St. Quentin, and thus ensured a yearly crop of babies.

A likelier explanation for the increase in population was a change in the climate. Northern Europe was perceptibly warmer around 800 A.D. than it had been in preceding centuries. The glaciers receded all over Scandinavia. There was more land that could be used for crops or pasture. The winters were shorter and milder. So decisive a factor was winter in the life of northern countries that the Vikings counted time not in years but in winters.

A long cold winter would mean that the provisions put away in the fall might run out while the weather was still too severe to replenish them by hunting or fishing, and then the weak, the old and the very young would die. Gentler winters meant that more babies would survive, more would grow up to swell the active, turbulent pool of younger sons who—since the property generally went to the oldest—were landless, foot-loose, bursting with energy and ready for any adventure.

The warm winters also provided the Norsemen of the Eighth and Ninth Centuries with an unusually protein-rich diet—their herds of cattle and flocks of sheep prospered, and more fish could be caught. This made the Vikings bigger and stronger, which gave them a considerable advantage over their adversaries. European chroniclers tended to see them as positive Goliaths: "Never did I see a people so gigantic," wrote the Arab traveler Ibn Fadlan; "they are tall as palm trees." That was an exaggeration. But male skeletons in Scandinavian graveyards of the period average five feet eight inches, an impressive height for the time, when few people stood taller than five feet five.

The sagas had a more imaginative explanation for the Vikings' advance on the world than diet and climate. Snorri Sturluson, the 13th Century Icelander who set down a collection of sagas recounting the reigns of gods and kings from the beginning of time to his own day, ascribed the migration of the Vikings to the bloody deeds of Harald Fairhair, first known as Harald Halfdanson.

Around 860 he inherited a minor kingdom upon the death of his father and vowed not to groom his shaggy head until he had brought to heel a handful of jarls who contested his right to rule. The jarls did not yield meekly. One, named Herlaug, had himself buried alive in a funeral mound rather than submit to Harald. Those who seized their swords and summoned their retainers did so only to die on the battlefield. One by one a number of others found resistance futile and followed the example

Survival gear for a murderous age

"No man should stir one step from where his weapons are, for he can never know when he might have use of them." So cautioned an ancient poem. In the violent Viking age a prudent man kept his weapons at hand, whether he was a farmer wary of a blood feud, a trader anxious about robbers, or a slave owner in fear of his chattel.

Although the Norsemen used bows and arrows in battle, they preferred spears, swords and axes. Spears were deadly at both long and short range, and the sagas memorialize feats of spearmanship. A Christianized warrior named Tryggvi won everlasting fame when, after being mocked as a priest's son, he hurled a shower of spears at his pagan foes, using both hands and roaring, "That is how my father taught me to say Mass!"

But the Vikings' greatest weapons were their heavy swords and trusty battle-axes that could crash through shields and armor and slay a man in one blow. Though Viking armorers produced steel, the finest blades were forged by craftsmen of Germany and France, and were treasured items of plunder and trade. Such weapons acquired their own personalities with names like "Leg-biter," the "Fierce" and "Long-and-sharp," and were lovingly handed down from father to son.

SHIELD

SWORD   SPEARHEAD

Viking weapons ranged from a functional wooden shield and an iron spearhead to an elaborate tunic of chain mail and an ornamental battle-ax inlaid with a silver design of a sinuous beast.

MAIL TUNIC

BATTLE-AX HEAD

of Herlaug's brother Hrollaug, going on their knees to Harald. Then, the tale continues, the King called for his scissors and comb, had his long yellow locks cut off—and emerged from the barber as Harald Fairhair.

For all its fanciful detail, the lively tale reflects the historical fact that some time around 872—almost 100 years after the raid on Lindisfarne—Harald Fairhair established the first centralized rule over the disparate settlements scattered throughout the hills and valleys of Norway, wresting from dozens of chieftains their lands and their time-honored independent rule over local provinces. In the near century that had elapsed since the plundering of Lindisfarne, the wide-ranging Viking ships had brought home more than booty from their expeditions abroad; together with silver and gold came Christian fashions of cropped hair and centralized rule.

The saga does not end there. It only begins. Some of the nobles, too proud to bow to Harald, loving life too much to resort to the funeral mound, found another way of evading Harald's unwelcome aspirations. They loaded their ships with their wives, children, followers, cattle, slaves and household goods, sailed across the sea, and settled on new land. And indeed, archeologists can date the appearance of Viking colonies on the Shetlands, the Orkneys and Iceland to the last third of the Ninth Century—the very time when Harald Fairhair was consolidating his power as king of Norway.

Typical of the bondi who raided, invaded and colonized abroad was one Egil Skallagrimsson, the 10th Century hero of a popular saga. His raiding expeditions were carried out pitilessly; the saga is a series of gleeful accounts of triumph over the weak and the gullible.

Egil was "exceeding ugly and like his father, black of hair," says the saga. Notwithstanding that disclaimer, the eye of the Viking beheld him as a thing of beauty. He was a fearless fighter, a loyal friend, a colossal toper who could empty one oxhorn full of ale after another without passing out, and a daredevil who could keep his wits about him in the worst of predicaments.

Right from the start he showed promise. He quaffed when he was three and committed manslaughter at seven. In a tiff over a ball game with a youngster named Grim, "Egil became wroth and heaved up the bat and smote Grim," killing his playmate, according to the saga. Servants and relatives came up with loud cries, and before the fracas was over, seven men were dead. Egil's mother, clearly the proper helpmeet for a Viking male, pronounced her son to be "of Viking stuff" and said that, "as soon as he had age thereto," the family should fit him out with "fleet keel and fair oars to fare abroad with Vikings" and "hew a man or twain."

He was only 12 when the wish of his mother's heart was granted. In due course he was to be found leading Viking expeditions across the far seas. Coming ashore with a dozen followers in a region known as Kurland, in modern Latvia, Egil scoured the countryside, slaying hither and yon and filling his ships with spectacular hauls of treasure. But an adventure would be no adventure at all without narrow escapes, and Egil had plenty of those.

In a clash one night with a Kurland farmer and a troop of followers, Egil and his comrades were overwhelmed by vastly superior numbers

Scowling menacingly, the legendary Viking warrior hero Egil Skallagrimsson brandishes his sword in this fanciful 17th Century Icelandic painting, which shows him dressed in the dandified garb of a much later era. Egil was a poet of note as well, and once wrote a 25-stanza ode, lamenting the drowning of his son.

and taken prisoner. The farmer wanted to execute them all on the spot, but his son, a bloodthirsty lad, argued that it would be more pleasant to wait till morning when they could see the expression on the faces of the men as they were being tortured. The farmer agreed, and the prisoners were fettered and thrown into an outbuilding while the Kurlanders went off to a victory feast.

Egil's giant hulk had impressed his captors, and they had bound him hand and foot to a thick upright pole. But as soon as he and his friends were left unguarded, he used his strength to twist and tug at the pole until he was able to yank it out of the ground and could work his way free from it. He untied the ropes on his hands with his teeth, and then unshackled his feet and freed his companions. They began to explore the property. In another building they heard cries from under their feet, pried loose some boards and discovered three Danish Vikings who had been taken prisoner during a raiding expedition the year before and had been kept as slaves on the farm. With these new recruits to guide them, Egil and his men found their way to the Kurlanders' treasure room and stripped it bare.

The men thought they had had enough adventure and profit for one day's foray, but Egil objected that it was not warrior-like to slip away in the dark: "We have stolen the farmer's property and he does not know it. Let us return to the farmstead and tell people what has been going on." The others refused to listen to him and went back to their ship.

Egil returned alone. Coming upon a fire, he picked up one of the logs, carried it to the hall where the Kurlanders were carousing, and thrust it under the eaves of the roof. The roof caught fire, and brands began falling on the banquet table. As the building burned, most of the befuddled Kurlanders died where they sat; those who tried to push their way out the door fell under Egil's ax. When they were all dead, Egil marched back to the ship and claimed, and got, the lion's share of the booty.

He then moved on, making additional and always profitable raids along the way on the coasts of Denmark, Holland, England, Sweden and Norway. Finally, as the years passed, even Egil began to feel old and tired and returned to a farm in Iceland, where he took up the life of a wealthy bondi on his land.

He lived on to be a feeble, crippled, blind old man, huddling by the fire, ignored by his kinfolk, scolded by cooks and servant girls for getting in their way. But the Viking fires burned on in Egil to the end. He went out riding one day with two slaves and his chests of silver. He came back alone and never said a word of what had become of the slaves or the silver: presumably he had buried the lot.

Later that year Egil died and was buried with his weapons. Generations passed, and some outsized human bones were dug up and were generally believed to be Egil's. The skull was remarkably large and heavy. It was set on a churchyard wall, and someone decided to test its hardness by swinging at it with the reverse side of his ax. "But the skull neither dented nor split," relates the saga. "It only turned white, and from that anybody could guess that that skull would not have been easily injured by the blows of small fry when it still had skin and flesh on it."

Such was the stuff of the Vikings.

Long-lost evidence of the shipwright's genius

The Viking sagas, so often laconic in chronicling the deeds of men, grow eloquent in describing the vessels in which the Norsemen set out to win the world. One saga relates how "gold shone on the prows and silver flashed on the variously shaped ships. So great, in fact, was the magnificence of the fleet that, if its lord had desired to conquer any peoples, the ships alone would have terrified the enemy."

Yet it has been only within the last 100 years, as archeologists have probed into the large burial mounds scattered up and down the Scandinavian coastline, that the world has gained any concrete knowledge of the Vikings' ships. For the Vikings, supreme seafarers that they were, carried their ships with them to the grave for use in the next world. A few of these have been uncovered in a near-miraculous state of preservation after a millennium in the earth.

Of the fabled gold and silver, alas, there was none. Possibly, grave robbers carried it off centuries before. Yet the ships themselves were ample enough testimony to the Viking shipbuilders' genius: long, lean, marvelously crafted and obviously seaworthy vessels of a sort never seen before, with astonishingly few components—keel, stem, stern, ribs and a dozen or so strakes on each side.

Two of these ships, one found at Gokstad, Norway, the other at nearby Oseberg, show different aspects of Viking shipbuilding. While the Gokstad ship (pages 37 and 39) was clearly a warship, the Oseberg ship (at right) appears to have been intended as a ceremonial and short-range craft suited more for the coastal transportation of an important personage than for lengthy ocean voyages.

Experts base their judgment not on its size. At 71 feet, with a 17-foot beam and a depth of three feet from keel to gunwale, it was as large as many blue-water ships. Rather, there was a certain economy of construction, evidenced by a thin keel, a jointed stern and unshuttered oar holes, that indicated light duty. The vessel, as would befit a Viking of wealth, was also superbly carved from curled stem to stern with an intricate frieze depicting stylized animals struggling up from the water line. Wrote one historian: "No one who has ever looked at the Oseberg ship herself can ever again think of the Ninth Century Norsemen as completely vile and soulless barbarians."

The swan-necked prow of the Oseberg ship rises 16 feet above the deck in the vaulted halls of the Viking Ships Museum in Oslo, Norway, where the 1,100-year-old vessel stands as a monument to the skill and artistry of the craftsmen who built it. The racks mounted at either gunwale hold the 30 oars that were deployed through the oar holes cut in both sides of the ship.

Inquiry into an earthy vault

In the early new year of 1880, some country people on the Gokstad farm in Sandar, Norway, started poking into a large barrow of earth that since time out of mind had been known as the King's Mound. It stood on a flat, treeless plain and was understood to be the tomb of a great Viking king. No one had dared disturb the mound before, but now curiosity got the better of superstition.

News of the venture spread to Oslo, where the government wisely decided not to let the excavation go unsupervised. The project was placed under the direction of an eminent Norwegian antiquarian, N. Nicolaysen—and not a moment too soon. Two days after Nicolaysen arrived on the scene, the prow of a huge wooden ship was unearthed.

The enormous oaken craft was the first complete Viking ship ever uncovered. Its wood had not rotted away because most moisture had been sealed out by a dense covering of blue clay packed around the vessel. When the Oseberg ship was discovered nearly 20 years later, it too owed its preservation to the blue clay.

Both ships were in need of repair; however, the weight of the clay and earth had fractured numerous ribs and strakes. The vessels were disassembled and treated with alum to give the wood extra hardness. The timbers were then joined together again. At last, when all was complete, the ships were saturated with linseed oil and finally sealed with two coats of heavy marine spar varnish.

The filigreed stern of the Oseberg ship emerges from the bed of Norwegian blue clay in which it has rested for centuries. The planking of the ship's port side, missing from the excavated vessel, would have been rabbeted into the groove along the inside of the sternpost.

A millennium's sleep underground has left this large sleigh from the Oseberg ship badly fractured but still recognizable. Its two sections, the elaborately chiseled riding box and the undercarriage with wooden runners, were held together with the rope shown here entwining them.

Under the intent scrutiny of a party of genteel onlookers, the exhumers of the Ninth Century Gokstad ship carefully chip clay away from the side planking. The burial chamber is visible behind the mast.

The Gokstad ship: a fighting craft supreme

At 76 feet from stem to stern and 17½ feet in the beam, the Gokstad ship was only a bit larger than the ceremonial Oseberg ship. Yet she is believed to have been a very efficient Viking longship, as the Norsemen called their warships.

Spare of any ornamentation and protected by a higher freeboard, she was trimmer and more durably crafted than the less seaworthy Oseberg ship. Her great keel—cut from a single oak trunk 80 feet long—was intentionally bowed amidships so that in battle she could be spun about virtually on her own axis. Yet with 16 oars on a side, she was only a medium-sized warship compared with the vessels that, according to the sagas, mounted 35 oars on each side and must have reached over 150 feet in length.

Nevertheless, the Gokstad ship could go anywhere her masters desired—as was admirably demonstrated in 1893 by a Norwegian seafarer named Magnus Andersen. Captain Andersen commissioned the construction of an exact copy of the Gokstad ship and boldly sailed her across the Atlantic from Bergen to Newfoundland. The 3,000-mile trip took 27 days, and the vessel achieved speeds as high as 11 knots.

The 24-foot spruce-wood gangplank from the Gokstad ship, a section of which is shown here, was incised with notches for traction and was attached to the ship by means of a square hole at one end.

This baler was cut from a single piece of wood and was attached to a long handle, which enabled the Vikings to reach into any part of the hull through gaps in the floor boards intentionally left open.

As clean of line as a pair of nutshells, two small boats found at Gokstad show the same meticulous attention to lightness of weight and graceful shape as larger Viking vessels. The 21-foot craft in the foreground mounted two sets of oars. The other had three sets and was 31 feet long.

The swooping lines of the Gokstad ship's planking converge at the stem to form a beaklike prow that towered perhaps nine feet above the water line. Some of the 32 oar ports are visible on either side.

Chapter 2

Masters of wind and wave

eside the brooding forested slopes of Trondheim Fjord in the year 998, King Olaf Tryggvason ordered the construction of what he intended to be "the best and most costly ship ever made in Norway." She was called the *Long Serpent* and the name was aptly chosen. This greatest of dragon ships was to stretch more than 160 feet from her curved, monster-headed prow to her identically curved and serpentine tail. She was designed to carry 34 oars on each side, and she could transport hundreds of Vikings into battle. The bow and the stern were to be elaborately carved and gilded. The sails would be richly dyed, and brightly painted shields would hang on her sides.

Vast oak forests then covered much of southern Norway, but King Olaf's men had to search far and wide to find a tree tall and straight enough to provide the trunk that would become the massive 145-foot keel of this awesome ship. It took a small army of Viking shipwrights to procure the materials: splitting well-seasoned logs so that each plank was grained for maximum strength; searching out naturally formed oak and spruce elbows and arches for the ship's ribs and struts; turning spruce roots into tough, naturally fibrous ropes to bind the shell and frame together; fashioning iron rivets and nails, wooden pegs or tree-nails, and walrushide thongs.

With all in readiness, construction began on the hull, starting from the great keel up. The task of carving the beautifully curved stempost and sternpost was entrusted to a skilled prowwright called Thorberg. Once these were in place, the planks would be added, each one placed above the last. But before the planking process got under way, Thorberg was called back to his farm on urgent personal business. When he returned to the shipbuilding weeks later, he saw that the planking had been completed, and to his dismay, he discovered that the journeymen carpenters—awed by the great dragon ship's size—had planked her with boards so thick that the ship would be much too heavy and ungainly in the water: the whole project would be a disaster.

King Olaf, unaware of this crucial flaw, was admiring the sleek, towering lines of the huge warship as she stood in the stocks. And everybody said that never was seen so large and so beautiful a ship of war. Thorberg said not a word. The next morning, the King came to take another look at his masterpiece and fell into one of the flaming rages for which he was so well known. During the night, someone had gone up and down one side of the ship, cutting deep notches in all the planks. The masterpiece was

Huge and menacing, with a dragon head and a veritable castle amidships, the Viking longship was viewed by the English as the embodiment of evil in this fantastic illumination from a 10th Century chronicle. "The pagans from the northern regions came with ships to Britain like stinging hornets and spread on all sides like fearful wolves," lamented a scribe after a raid on a monastery.

ruined, raged the King. "The man shall die who has thus destroyed the vessel out of envy," he cried, "and I shall bestow a great reward on whoever finds him out."

Then up spoke Thorberg, the prowwright: "I will tell you, King, who did it. I did it myself."

"You must restore it all," swore the King, "to the same condition as before, or your life shall pay for it."

As the King stormed off, Thorberg picked up his ax and began chipping away at all the thick planks. He trimmed them down till their surfaces were even with the deepest of his notches. When King Olaf and his men came back and examined the shaved side of the ship, they were amazed and delighted.

As both Thorberg and Olaf well knew, the first principle of Viking ship construction was lightness and flexibility. The thinner the planks, the lighter the craft; the lighter she was the less water she would draw, so she could maneuver in shallow waters where heavier craft would most certainly run aground. Thinner planking also meant that a craft's sides could be built higher so that she could ride above taller seas—and so that Viking warriors aboard could hurl their spears down upon lower, more vulnerable vessels.

There were other advantages to thin planking. With a light but sturdy shell, a Viking ship could flex in the ocean waves like a slim leaf; the keel could bend up and down by as much as an inch, and the gunwales could twist as much as six inches out of true without doing any damage to the ship. This would enable the hull to bend to the waves and slip through them with the least amount of resistance, making the ship faster and more stable. In the most favorable wind, a typical Viking vessel could achieve speeds of well over 10 knots. And clearly, the *Long Serpent* could do even better.

For a man like King Olaf, who had led war bands most of his days, these were matters of life or death. He recognized the genius of Thorberg's alterations, and ordered the prowwright to trim down the other side of the ship as well. He then appointed him master builder for the entire project. Ever afterward, Thorberg proudly bore the nickname *Scafhogg*, or "Smoothing Stroke," and the mighty *Long Serpent* became the most famous dragon ship of all.

A terror to the outside world, the Viking longships—the biggest among them called dragons—were a source of great and understandable pride to Norsemen. At a time in the Dark Ages when the majority of men and women in the West lived and died within walking distance of their birthplaces, when travel was slow and dangerous, Vikings seemed to skitter over the map like water birds over a pond, appearing when they were least expected, disappearing when they chose. They could do this because, unlike the other peoples of Europe in the early Middle Ages, they understood the sea and the power that mastery of the sea could give. Out of their primordial fjords and silent forests, endless waterways and wave-swept islands, they were born to the sea and were soon seaborne—amphibious by nature and destined to become the quintessential seafarers of their age.

Sword upraised, King Olaf Tryggvason of Norway addresses a page after a victorious battle against the English at Maldon. Though converted to Christianity during his campaigns in England, Olaf forever remained a pagan in his soul. He filled his court with magicians and was himself a noted fortuneteller: ornithomancy—prophesying the future by observing the flight patterns of birds— was one of Olaf's favorite methods and earned him the nickname of "Crowbone."

"The Danes," observed an early medieval chronicler, "live in the sea"; it was scarcely an exaggeration, and it applied to the Swedes and the Norwegians as well. Long before they developed ships that were capable of traversing oceans, the Scandinavians depended upon the sea for food, fishing for cod, haddock, whiting, sardine, herring, tuna and mackerel. They ventured out ever farther from shore in their dugouts and skin boats and wooden craft of strange new shapes. And eventually domination of the sea was theirs because of the sheer excellence of their ship designs—and because of their ingenuity in devising unusual navigational methods.

The earliest Norse ships appear in rock carvings dating from around 1500 B.C.; the familiar high-curved stem and stern of the Scandinavian double-ender are clearly evident in these carvings, the inevitable result of the Vikings' having to negotiate the violent seas of the North. This form of double-ender, which was a uniquely Scandinavian design, permitted smooth handling of the ship even with a mountainous following sea because the wave force was divided by the stern as easily as it was by the bow, and the stern then lifted—keeping the craft from being pooped and possibly overwhelmed.

Although some of the earliest Bronze Age boats in northernmost Scandinavia were sewn together from skins stretched over oak frames, another construction technique appears to have been in use at the time in southern Norway. This was a peculiarly Norse invention, with the shell made not of skins but of very thin wooden planks lashed together by withies—finely drawn, sinewy spruce roots. At first, this wooden boat was constructed with no keel, because the added strength provided by a keel was not necessary when the ship was merely being rowed through the comparatively sheltered waterways and fjords, on the vast lakes, or through the endless archipelagoes of Sweden, Denmark and Norway. This lightweight craft could be beached easily, or she could be taken far up shallow rivers. Because of her high stem and stern, she could also venture out through surf and across broad bodies of water such as the Baltic or the Skagerrak during the better summer months. But for hundreds of years, she could go no farther. The Northmen had not yet devised sails, and about two days was as long as the weather was likely to remain calm enough for rowing.

This prototype of the longship exhibited numerous other shortcomings. She was too narrow, which gave her a precarious roll, and the sides were not high enough to give her sufficient freeboard for heavy North Atlantic swells. Without a keel, she was difficult to control if there was any adverse current or wind, and even the best oarsmen would be quickly exhausted trying to keep the ship from broaching in a storm. Thus, until the advent of the Viking age, this ingenious vessel remained an effective weapon for local blood feuds and a vehicle for coastal trade, but nothing more.

It was only during the Seventh Century that the Norsemen learned how to build and sail a longship: to take the finely hewn, neatly wrought prototype, incorporate a keel to add directional stability and thrust, step a sturdy mast, raise a single full-breasted sail and drive her forward beyond the horizon and into the vast expanse of the unknown ocean.

The critical addition was the sail, and how the Vikings acquired it is a mystery. The Roman Empire, with its sophisticated square-rigged merchantmen, had collapsed centuries earlier as the Dark Ages fell upon Europe. But it is possible that Scandinavian coastal traders observed crude sailing craft inherited by the Frisians from the Romans, whose empire once abutted on Frisia on the North Sea, or that Norse overland traders reaching the Black Sea admired the rigging of the Arab dhows they observed there.

But the Viking sail was so unusual that it might well have been developed in isolation. For a typical 90-foot longship the mast measured a stubby 30 feet—short enough to be lowered easily into two or three crutches fixed amidships, well out of the way during a landing or a fight at sea. The sail, to make up for what it lacked in height, was cut in an enormously wide rectangle—up to 40 or 50 feet across in a typical longship, perhaps more than 70 feet for the *Long Serpent*. It was hoisted aloft on a main yard and sometimes was footed to a secondary yard at its base. For efficiency when running before the wind, the sail would often be spread by two whisker poles, spars fitted into sockets in a pair of blocks mounted on each bulwark just forward of the mast. When the vessel was sailing across the wind or into it—and Viking longships by all accounts sailed well into the wind—only one of these whisker poles would be used.

The sails themselves were woven of coarse wool in a double layer to provide strength. Their color was generally red—sometimes solid, sometimes patterned in diamonds, squares or stripes, the better to announce one's presence to friends. Great power could be obtained from these sails. But when they were wet they became exceedingly heavy, and in storms or in fluky winds they could be difficult to maneuver and actually deadly: even a strapping Viking chieftain could be knocked from his feet; the Norwegian King Eystein, for one, was toppled off his longship and drowned by a wildly swinging yard from another ship that was sailing alongside.

At the same time that the Norsemen began stepping masts and rigging sails, they also began building true oak keels into their ships for the extra strength required to take the stresses of ocean travel and the driving force of the mast under sail. The keel was T-shaped; experience had shown that such a keel cut the water and helped the helmsman maintain an even course through contrary seas. Because Vikings needed to beach their boats and to battle in shallow waters as well as to cross oceans, they kept their keels shallow, but made up for that by extending them from stem to stern.

The Vikings also devised a remarkable rudder. A stubby, modified steering oar, it was fixed to the starboard quarter of the craft on a large block of wood pegged so the oar would turn as a lever turns on a fulcrum; the helmsman used a tiller bar. Since the Norse word for steering board was *stjornbordi*, the rudder lent its name to the starboard, or right, side of the boat.

No longer confined to their own coasts, producing ever-larger, beamier, more weatherly longships—their sides planked higher to keep

Vessels for every sea and goal

Though all Viking vessels were basically alike—double ended, constructed with overlapping planks of oak, and powered by oars and a single square sail—they evolved into a variety of sizes and shapes designed to meet different objectives and conditions at sea. Obviously, in a day of handcraftsmanship without formalized plans, no two vessels were built exactly the same. Nevertheless, by about the year 1000 four designs had emerged as the standard hulls of the Viking era.

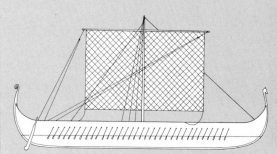

The pride of kings and the flagship of the Viking fleet, the great drakar, or dragon ship, measured more than 160 feet in length and about 25 feet across the beam, and was equipped with as many as 72 oars. Aside from her enormous size, the most notable feature of the drakar was an extra-high freeboard, which gave the 300-man crew of warriors as great an advantage as possible when engaged in combat.

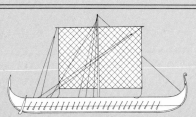

Built low for speed and ease in handling, the longship was the most versatile of Viking craft, used both for raiding (with up to 200 men) and coastal trading (around 20 tons of cargo). Generally about 100 feet long and 20 feet in the beam, she had ports to accommodate about 50 oars.

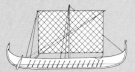

Smaller than the warships, the karve served as a utility craft for the fleet and as a chieftain's pleasure yacht during peacetime. About 70 feet long with a beam of some 17 feet and ports for 16 oars, she had a draft of less than three feet—shallow enough to travel almost anywhere.

The only Viking vessel to rely primarily on sails rather than oars, the knarr was brilliantly designed for commerce and exploration instead of war. Her short (54 foot), beamy (15 foot) hull could carry 15 tons of cargo, and her deep keel let her track a steady course out of sight of land.

Two Ninth Century silver coins convey the dual purpose of Viking activity. On the coin at right, a high-prowed warship bears on its gunwales the shields of raiders; the left coin depicts a peaceable trading vessel cruising along with her sail reefed.

them dry while they heeled across the storm-tossed North Sea—the Norsemen were at last loosed upon the world.

The exhilaration and sense of bold accomplishment the Northmen felt on the sea was never better described than in the Eighth Century epic poem *Beowulf* when Prince Beowulf of the Scandinavian tribe called Weder-Gēatas sets sail to help a Danish ally, Hrothgar, in his fight against the monster, Grendel:

Over breaking billows, with bellying sail
And foamy beak, like a flying bird
The ship sped on, till the next day's sun
Showed sea cliffs shining, towering hills
And stretching headlands. The sea was crossed,
The voyage ended, the vessel moored.
And the Weder people waded ashore
With clatter of trappings and coats of mail;
Gave thanks to God that His Grace had granted
Seapaths safe for the ocean journey.

Aside from the fact that the narrative was transcribed by a Christian monk in Northumbria, and that the Vikings at the time were still heathens who were not inclined to express gratitude to a Christian God, the phrases resound with love for the sea, and with the virility and prowess that the Vikings derived from being masters of these incomparable warships.

So much were the ships a part of their self-image that the Vikings decorated and caparisoned each longship to display wealth, rank and power, at once impressing their friends and allies and awing their enemies. When a fleet of longships commanded by King Svein Forkbeard prepared to set sail from Denmark to invade England in 1013, a chronicler fell into Homeric rhapsody over the sight of so many ornately carved and gilded vessels:

"On one side lions moulded in gold were to be seen on the ships, on the other birds on the tops of the masts indicated by their movements the winds as they blew, or dragons of various kinds poured fire from their nostrils. Here there were glittering men of solid gold or silver nearly comparable to live ones, there bulls with necks raised high and legs outstretched were fashioned leaping and roaring like live ones. The sides of the ships were not only painted with ornate colours, but were covered with gold and silver figures. The royal vessel excelled the others in beauty as much as the king preceded the soldiers in the honour of his proper dignity. Placing their confidence in such a fleet, when the signal was suddenly given, the warriors set out gladly and, as they had been ordered, placed themselves round about the royal vessel with level prows, some in front and some behind. The blue water might be seen foaming far and wide, and the sunlight, cast back in the gleam of metal, spread a double radiance in the air."

However much he loved fighting and warships, the Viking lived on the sea for many other reasons as well, and devised vessels to match his needs. When he turned his genius for design and construction from warships to ships for long-distance trade and exploration—and, eventually, for emigration to the farthest reaches of the ocean—he produced a boat equally extraordinary: stouter and sturdier, designed to brave the worst seas in search of landfalls far beyond any other Westerners' wildest dreams.

These were the *hafskip*—*haf* meaning the ocean, and *skip*, of course, meaning ship. The hafskip was built with the same construction methods as the fighting langskip—high-curved stem and stern and lapstrake planking—but it was only half as long. And the hafskip was by its very nature more seaworthy. The longship was built as an instrument of combat; long, narrow and lined with oars for close-quarter maneuvering, it had little room for cargo. The hafskip, by contrast, was built to carry dozens of men and women, plus all their belongings and provisions, for a period of weeks or even months at sea.

To accommodate these passengers and considerable cargo, the hafskip was designed to be deep and beamy, with stouter ribs and thicker planks and a higher freeboard to keep waves from washing over the sides in northern ocean storms. Compared with the light and flexible longship, the hafskip was a heavy-displacement vessel; in light airs the longship was faster because it took a good wind to press a heavily laden hafskip up to her maximum hull speed. But once out in the violent gales of the North Atlantic the hafskip was at home. In towering seas and howling winds, where a longship might be forced beyond the limitations of its design, the hafskip remained secure, driving through the seas at speeds of 10 knots and more.

There were a few oar positions in the bow and stern quarters, but only to stroke in and out of fjords and other narrow anchorages. The foredeck and afterdeck were planked over, and there was a substantial hold amidships. Cargo was piled everywhere, and covered with oxhides. Sometimes the ship's boat, a simple lapstrake rowboat, was carried on board, sometimes towed behind.

These admirable hafskip were built in two basic forms: the stubby *byrdingr*, which was a small vessel—generally less than 40 feet long— used for coastal trading, and the somewhat larger *knarr*, which was about 50 feet in length and 15 feet in the beam. It was this knarr that became the great Viking ocean voyager, and the care and maintenance of this stout-hearted vessel preoccupied everyone who was fortunate enough to serve as its master.

In a 13th Century compendium of Norse lore called the *King's Mirror*, a father gives his son some advice about the upkeep and proper handling of an oceangoing knarr: "If you are preparing to carry on trade beyond the seas and you sail your own ship, have it thoroughly coated with tar in the autumn and, if possible, keep it tarred all winter. But if the ship is placed on timbers too late to be coated in the fall, tar it when spring opens and let it dry thoroughly afterward. Always buy shares in good vessels or in none at all. Keep your ship attractive, for then capable men will join you, and it will be well manned. Be sure to have your ship ready when summer begins and do your traveling while the season is best. Keep reliable tackle on shipboard at all times, and never remain out at sea in late autumn, if you can avoid it."

A glorious send-off into a glorious hereafter

"A King is for glory, not for long life," cried a Norwegian chieftain named Magnus Bareleg as he prepared to meet his gods while fighting in a raid on Ireland. For the Vikings, death after a lifetime of glorious combat was presumed to be the start of an even more glorious hereafter of feasting and fighting in Valhalla. And the elaborate Viking burial rites, reconstructed on these pages, made certain that the Norse heroes departed this earth with everything they could need in the next world.

In the drawing below, the ship of the dead chief has been placed in a huge grave perhaps 60 yards long and 50 yards wide; workmen on the funeral ship hurry to complete a sturdy burial chamber made of timbers and adorned with tapestry. A slave girl belonging to the dead hero will be sacrificed in order to accompany her master, who lies inside the chamber on a fine large bed. Surrounding him are the accoutrements necessary for both combat and comfort in the hereafter: his sword, ax and shield, an ironbound chest of clothes, an extra cloak, and oaken buckets containing such foods as apples and walnuts.

Equipping the hero for his otherworldly voyage

As the burial arrangements for the Viking chieftain continue, a vast amount of equipment is put aboard the longship. Servants trundle a pony cart across a gangplank while a sleigh for winter travel stands on the bank in the right foreground. Men behind the cart are carrying boxes of dishes. A number of household articles have already been brought on board and are being placed near the mast: a wooden bowl, buckets, an iron cooking cauldron and a cask, which could be used for the crew to drink from.

The roughly hewn burial chamber has now been completely enclosed in order to keep the chieftain and his slave

dry and comfortable during the long voyage that lies ahead.

The prow of the vessel points in the direction of the sea, and the whole craft is braced in an upright position by heavy supports. The pair of wooden forks fastened to the side of the ship will be used to hold oars. At the raised poop lies the anchor, which will be dropped when the chieftain reaches his destination. On the far side at the stern, workers with wooden spades complete the job of excavation while the men on the bank above them carry more goods to be placed in the grave. Just to their left are two small boats of 26 and 21 feet, which will be placed on board as well, in case

they are needed during the voyage. Near the boats an ostler leads a horse on board, for it would not do for the Viking chief to be left on foot in the next world. Other horses and an ox await their turn to board.

When everything is in readiness, the sacrifices of animals will begin. Among the animals to be killed will be the exotic peacock, already fanning its tail on deck. This bird attests to the high rank of the chieftain. Unknown in the wild state in Scandinavia, the peacock was native to India and could have been procured only with great difficulty and for great treasure from Muslim traders who had access to the East.

Burying the great craft and its captain

The sacrifices completed, workers begin to bury the funeral ship in this view of the stern, shoveling in a layer of sand and blue clay. Carpenters have chopped off the mast so that it will not rise above the burial mound.

Once the ship is covered with sand and clay, layers of moss and twigs will follow, and finally a top layer of peat sods will be added to make the mound virtually airtight. At the very last, beautifully carved wooden memorial posts, the Viking equivalent of gravestones, will be set up to mark the boundaries of the grave site—and the Viking hero will be well launched on his way to glory in Valhalla.

The father continues: "Whenever you travel at sea, keep on board two or three hundred ells"—since an ell then measured over 18 inches, this meant about 330 to 500 feet—"of wool of a sort suitable for mending sails, if that should be necessary, a large number of needles, and a supply of thread and cord. You will always need to carry a supply of nails, both spikes and rivets, of such sizes as your ship demands; also good boat hooks and broadaxes, gouges and augers, and all such other tools as ship carpenters make use of. All these things that I have now named you must remember to carry with you on shipboard, whenever you sail on a trading vessel and the ship is your own."

The conversation between father and son then turns from maintenance and equipment to questions of prudent seamanship. The son inquires when—how early in spring and how late in fall—it is possible to make such a voyage. "The seas are not all alike," answers the father, "nor are they all of equal extent. Small seas have no great perils, and one may risk crossing them at almost any time; for one has to make sure of fair winds to last a day or two only, which is not difficult for men who understand the weather. But where travel is beset with greater perils, whether because the sea is wide and full of dangerous currents, or because the prow points toward shores where the harbors are rendered insecure by rocks, breakers, shallows or sandbars—whenever the situation is such, one needs to use great caution; and no one should venture to travel over such waters when the season is late. It seems to me that one should hardly venture overseas later than the beginning of October. For at that time the sea begins to grow very restless, and the tempests always increase in violence as autumn passes and winter approaches. Men may venture out upon almost any sea except the largest as early as the beginning of April. For after the 16th of March, the days lengthen, the sun rises higher, and the nights grow shorter."

The author adds sagely: "The man who is to be a trader will have to brave many perils, sometimes at sea and sometimes in heathen lands, but nearly always among alien peoples; and it must be his constant purpose to act discreetly wherever he happens to be. On the sea he must be alert and fearless."

The Norse gods who ruled the sea provided an excellent reason for caution. Aegir and his wife Ran were personifications of the ocean's capacity for good and ill. When properly propitiated, Aegir could offer up the riches of the sea, but when angered, he could make even the stoutest Viking quail. In *Fridthjofs Saga* it was suggested that the wise sailor should always carry a piece of gold, so that if caught in a storm he would not be empty-handed when he drowned and came into the presence of Aegir's wife. He could cross her palm with gold, thus assuring his entrance into Valhalla. A good captain was supposed to see to it that all his men had this offering of gold—even if it meant distributing it from his own purse.

Aegir's nine daughters were the waves of the sea, called by such forbidding names as Howler and Grasper, and no Viking wanted to spend a night in their arms.

The thunder god Thor also needed to be placated by Vikings at sea

because he controlled the climate, and whether a sailor ended up in the grips of Aegir or Ran and their daughters often depended upon Thor's having been appeased by sacrifices before the voyage or proper oaths from the helmsman's position.

In addition to the hazards of the weather, ocean voyages posed more prosaic problems, particularly when knarrs were venturing out loaded with emigrants on a colonizing expedition to the countless islands off the coasts of Scotland, to the shores of Ireland or, later, to the new-found lands across the wild northern waters.

That the Vikings succeeded in these epic voyages was attributable not only to their magnificent blue-water sailing vessels. They were superlative navigators as well—venturing boldly out to explore the unknown, and then repeating their voyages almost casually, with a certainty of direction that was nothing short of phenomenal. What lay behind all Viking seafaring was the Norseman's instinct for the sea, a sense that seemed uncanny to the landsman, but it was in reality a prodigious body of hard-earned knowledge accumulated throughout centuries of nautical life.

The Viking drew great meaning from the look of cloud formations, from changes in winds and wave patterns, from ocean currents and ground swells, from sea fogs, water colors and temperatures. He could read information from the habits of sea birds, was alert to the over-water migration of certain land birds, and tracked the movements of fish and whales that came down from the north. A seasoned Viking navigator could tell when he was approaching the Faroe Islands by the swell building up over the banks surrounding the group. He would know he was nearing Greenland because of the abrupt change in the temperature

Norway's King Olaf Tryggvason sends a smashing blow to the shoulder of a sea ogress, one of the legendary perils of the deep lying in wait for seafaring Vikings. This terrifying creature, relates a saga, had "shoulders like a horse, but behind all like a serpent, with a monstrous great coil and broad tail," which she used to awful effect, "putting her hands on one side and her tail under the ship and up on the other so that the ship is capsized."

of the water as he entered the polar current, by the pronounced change in the water's color from ocean blue to green, and by the occasional presence of drift ice.

The Vikings were masters of the relentless currents that swirled around in the North Atlantic and arctic waters. The Norwegian Current surged powerfully up the coast of Norway toward the Lofoten Islands, tending to carry ships in its path speedily toward Iceland. From Iceland, ships setting a westward course were carried along by the Irminger Current and then whisked southward by the Greenland Current; finally they were propelled down the coast of North America by the Labrador Current.

Prevailing winds generally helped them on their way as well, blowing northward between Norway and Iceland, and southward between Iceland and Greenland. The elaborately decorated wind vanes mounted on the prows and mastheads of Viking ships testify to the sailors' keen sensitivity to every errant puff, for it was only by taking full advantage of both the wind and the currents that rapid ocean passages could be made without tragedy.

In a later day mariners would have magnetic compasses and sophisticated speed-measuring devices to help them navigate with precision. But in Viking times the compass had not yet reached Western Europe from the Orient. As for computing speed, the only way the Vikings might have managed that would have been to toss a chip of wood into the sea and count how long it took to travel the vessel's length to the stern or by watching bubbles float by.

Viking seafarers employed a primitive celestial navigation to help them measure course and distance. At night, Polaris, the North Star, was the primary heavenly indicator. This star was usually visible overhead, circling tightly around the pole below, and thus a boon beyond price to mariners. On clear nights, it required only a method of determining the angle of Polaris off the bow to determine a rough course. By holding a steady 90° angle from Polaris, for example, the Vikings could be sure that they were heading directly east or west. In later years this would be known as latitude sailing—and its ramifications for the Vikings were enormous, particularly on their great western voyages of exploration and trade across hundreds of miles of open ocean.

No one venturing down the coast of Scandinavia could fail to notice, as well, that the altitude of Polaris from the horizon would decrease as the vessel sailed southward, and that the reverse would hold true on a northward journey. Thus by measuring the altitude of this star, Viking navigators could determine with considerable accuracy how far north or south they had traveled.

Employing the sun as a navigational tool was somewhat more complex. In the depths of winter, when the sun scarcely rose at all, it was useless as a directional beacon. But then only the most foolhardy Viking ventured far from land at that time of year, with its bitter cold and monstrous storms. In the summertime, however, when the sun was above the horizon for a great part of the day and night, the Vikings made full use of it.

As was the case with Polaris, the height of the sun as it arced across the sky would change as the vessel sailed south or north. On a southerly heading, the altitude of the sun would increase, and the reverse would also hold true on a northerly course. The sun could also indicate direction as it traveled from east to west. To measure these values and apply them to navigation, the Vikings devised three ingenious navigational instruments that they called the sun board, the sunstone and the sun shadow board. The sun board appears to have been a bearing dial (*page 55*) on which were marked compass points, radiating from a hole in the center. With the help of a pointer mounted on the dial, the Vikings were able to take a course bearing from the sun as it rose in the east or set in the west and to maintain any course simply by checking this crude triangulation each day. From Viking accounts it is known that Norse navigators were accustomed also to taking a sighting at noon when the sun reached the north-south meridian. Thus, although he had no magnetic compass, the Viking could make a reasonably accurate determination of his compass bearings each day.

Under overcast skies or in dense fog, the Viking made use of a remarkable calcite mineral crystal named cordierite, the Norse sunstone, found in Scandinavia and Iceland. When a crystal of cordierite is held at right angles to the plane of polarized light from the sun, the crystal instantly changes from yellow to dark blue. Probably first used as a decorative element in Norse jewelry, the sunstone was a real boon to Viking seafarers. Even in a thick fog or under a woolen sky, a navigator in mid-ocean could locate the exact position of the invisible sun by rotating a chunk of cordierite until it suddenly turned dark blue. Since it produced the same color change even when the sun was as much as 7° below the horizon, the navigator could continue to take sightings after sunset.

But for general course settings during daylight hours, the Vikings relied most heavily on the sun shadow board. This device, which allowed them to determine their latitude and then sail along that latitude over vast ocean reaches to their destination, appears to have been a wooden disc marked with concentric circles that were the rough equivalent of latitudes. In the center of the disc was a vertical staff, similar to the one on a sundial, that could be pushed up and down to make it taller or shorter according to the position of the sun in the sky. When the staff was set at the proper height for the sun's declination in mid-August, for example, the shadow cast by the sun at noon, when it reached its zenith, would fall on a particular circle. By keeping the sun's shadow on that same circle each noon, the navigator could maintain his latitude; if the shadow fell to one side of the circle or the other, the helmsman could tell how much he should steer north or south to get back on course. To keep the instrument level at sea, a sailor was assigned to hold it floating in a bowl of water.

The sun shadow board became the heart of Viking daylight latitude sailing, and all directions given to Norse navigators concerned themselves with reckonings to and from pivotal points of geography where latitude sailing could begin. A vessel would sail roughly north or south until it reached a pivotal point, and then it would sail east or west to its destination—or to another pivotal point. The Norsemen were aided

With notches to mark points from north around the horizon, this fragment of a circular bearing dial from the 13th Century is thought to be a part of a crude hand-held celestial navigation device used by the Vikings. A shaft went through the circular hole, and a movable pointer overlaid the dial; on clear nights, by sighting along the pointer at the North Star, navigators could get their bearings—and thus their course—from true north.

Fashioned of gilt bronze, an elaborately crafted 11th Century Viking weather vane depicts a mythological animal standing atop openwork in which fantastic beasts lie entangled in a mesh of serpent-like tendrils. Mounted in the bows or on the mastheads of Viking ships, such indicators provided precise bearings on the wind, thus enabling the helmsman to maintain the most efficient sailing angle.

enormously by the location of Scandinavia. The latitude of the Horns in Iceland was the same as that of Trondheim Fjord in Norway; from Bergen, Norway, a ship could sail on the same latitude to the Shetland Islands and Cape Farewell in Greenland; the Orkney Islands were on the same latitude as Stavanger, Norway. By holding to any given Polaris angle or sun shadow length for the duration of the voyage, a Viking sailor could maintain his prescribed course to within just a few miles of his destination. At that point he could watch for natural phenomena—perhaps a darker variety of the fulmar petrel known to inhabit the waters around southern Iceland; or an increase in puffins, which would indicate the proximity of the Faroe Islands with their vast colonies of sea birds. One of the sagas tells of a ship's crew that "drifted southward across the ocean so that they had birds from Ireland." And as they approached Greenland, they could recognize the iceblink, or reflection in the sky of the ice cap.

Thus did the Vikings construct their magnificent ships, and for centuries navigate them by sun and star across the northern seas and oceans. The Western world would not see mariners to equal or surpass them until the Middle Ages passed into the Renaissance and Portugal's Prince Henry the Navigator ushered in the great age of exploration at the close of the 15th Century.

And what of the *Long Serpent?* What fate befell that great vessel, the epitome of Viking design, the pride of shipwright Thorberg, the joy of Norway's King Olaf Tryggvason? The record does not tell whether he took her on any overseas raids or ocean voyages. Possibly not, for he may have regarded her as too great a treasure to risk on such ventures. In fact, she seems to have been employed mainly as a royal vessel of state, to carry King Olaf on various ceremonial cruises around Scandinavian waters. And it is an irony of history that this was her role when she finally came to combat, and became a prize in one of the many ambushes and sea battles that pitted Viking fleet against Viking fleet throughout the age of the Norsemen.

This battle occurred scarcely two years after the *Long Serpent* was built in Trondheim Fjord. Olaf had made many enemies in the course of a long and bloody career, and his foes—Denmark's King Svein, Sweden's King Olaf and a disaffected Norwegian noble named Eirik—brought together their warriors and their fleets and plotted to lay a trap for the Norwegian monarch. The conspirators agreed that, if they were successful, they would divide the kingdom of Norway among themselves—and whosoever captured the prized *Long Serpent* could keep her as his own.

The Norwegian King was at the time cruising the southern Baltic in the *Long Serpent* with a fleet of 11 dragon ships and numerous smaller longships and supply vessels. He had gone to Rogaland, in southern Norway, to conclude the marriage of a sister to a local jarl, and following that was spending the summer renewing old acquaintances in Vindland, on the south coast of the Baltic.

When all was in readiness to carry out the ruse, Olaf's enemies prepared to lure him into their ambush. They dispatched a Viking named

Churning up great curling wakes, two longships sweep across the sea under sail in this 14th Century Danish church fresco. The scene supposedly illustrates a legendary 11th Century race to Norway from Sweden by Olaf Haraldsson in his ship, the Lazy Bear, and Harald Hardradi in the Joyful Serpent, with the Norwegian throne as the prize. Although such a race never occurred, Harald eventually did become the king of all Norway.

Sigvald, the ruler of an island off Vindland, to lead the unwitting Olaf astray. When the Norwegian fleet was ready to set sail for home, Sigvald persuaded Olaf in the *Long Serpent* to follow him on a devious journey through the unfamiliar waters: "For I know where the water is deepest between the islands and in the sounds, and these large ships require the deepest." The shallow-draft vessels of King Olaf's fleet, not requiring such deep waters, sailed into the Baltic.

The *Long Serpent* and a few escort ships followed Sigvald's vessel into the channel behind Svold Island near Vindland, where the combined enemy fleets waited in ambush. Watching from a hilltop on the island, Eirik and the Kings of Sweden and Denmark saw the parade of longships approach, and among them was one great ship with a large dragonhead richly gilded. The Danish King boasted: "That dragon shall carry me this evening high, for I shall steer it." But Earl Eirik, in a voice loud enough for many people to overhear, sneered, "If King Olaf had no other vessels except that one, King Svein would never take it from him with the Danish force alone." Indeed, the forces of the Swedish and the Danish Kings were to prove insufficient, and it was Earl Eirik who would seize the initiative in the battle.

The ambushers hurried down to their fleet and prepared their warriors for battle, striking tents and gathering weapons and shields.

As the *Long Serpent* neared Svold Island, the enemy fleet came rowing forth to the sound. In great alarm, King Olaf's escort converged on the *Long Serpent*, begging their ruler to flee if he could and not risk battle with so great a force. High on the afterdeck where he stood at the steering oar, King Olaf replied: "Strike the sails; never shall men of mine think of flight. I never fled from battle. Let God dispose of my life, but flight I shall never take."

Olaf's men then ordered all loyal ships to form the usual Viking line of battle: prow to prow, tail to tail, to be lashed together at stem and stern in such a way that they formed a great fortress-like raft (*pages 60-61*). But Olaf's ship was so huge in comparison with those on either side that her prow protruded far beyond the prows of the other ships. This posed a terrible hazard to King Olaf's leading warriors, who would be fighting in the prow of his dragon ship, and would thus be exposed on both sides.

"We shall have hard work of it here," grumbled Olaf's greatest prowman, Ulf the Red. The Norwegian King was furious at the complaint; he drew his bow and aimed an arrow at his own prowman, but Ulf responded, "Shoot another way, King, where it is more needful. My work is your gain."

From the enemy fleet King Svein was the first to reach the *Long Serpent*'s prow, but he suffered tremendous losses when he attempted to board. Then came the Swedish King, and he, too, was beaten off and sustained frightful casualties. But Earl Eirik was not to be thwarted. Attacking the flank with many ships, he worked his deadly way down the line of defenders, hewing and hacking each vessel clear of her warriors and then cutting her loose from the rest. Outnumbered and weakened, King Olaf's men began to panic. They clambered from their smaller ships to the bigger ones at the center of the line, their numbers growing fewer and fewer as they retreated before the attackers, until at last all the survivors were gathered aboard the *Long Serpent* herself.

The Norse poet Halldor described the carnage:

Sharp was the clang of shield and sword,
And shrill the song of spears on board.
And whistling arrows thickly flew
Against the Serpent's gallant crew.
And still fresh foemen, it is said,
Earl Eirik to her long side led;
Whole armies of his Danes and Swedes,
Wielding on high their blue sword blades.
Hard pressed on every side by foes,
The Serpent reels beneath the blows;
Crash go the shields around the bow!
Breastplates and breasts pierced thro' and thro'!

Surrounded and now doomed, Olaf and his men stood behind their shields as a hail of missiles from the enemy ships crashed down around them. When at last Eirik pulled alongside the *Long Serpent*, Einar Thambarskelfir—another of Olaf's brave men—drew himself up by the *Long Serpent*'s mast and tried to get a clear shot with his bow and arrow at Eirik. Einar's arrow hit the tiller above Eirik's head so hard, recounts the saga, that it drove into the wood up the length of its shaft. Einar drew his bow again, but an arrow from Eirik's ship hit his bow and split it in two.

"What is that," cried King Olaf, "that broke with such a noise?"

"Norway, King, from your hands," answered Einar.

Olaf threw him another bow, but Einar spurned it: "Too weak for the bow of a mighty king!" And he fought on instead with sword and shield.

King Olaf, who was hurling spears at the enemy, noticed his men were landing many blows with their swords but seldom making a fatal wound. They called to him that their swords were blunt after hours of battle. Olaf opened a chest and passed out sharp new swords—but as he did his men saw blood running down his arm and under his steel glove. He was wounded, but they could not tell where and dared not ask. Aboard the *Long Serpent* the toughest men were fighting in the bow and stern, where the ship was highest; in the center Olaf's men were thinned by slaughter. Using this gap, Eirik's Vikings stormed the *Long Serpent*.

At last there was only a small band of defenders gathered around King Olaf in the stern of his great ship. The deck was wet with blood. More and more of Eirik's men climbed aboard and closed on the stern, hacking with broadaxes and swords. When Olaf and his remaining men saw that the battle was lost, they leaped into the sea with their armor, shields and weapons. The enemy tried to seize the King before he sank. But he pulled his shield over his head and vanished beneath the waters.

The *Long Serpent* became Eirik's booty, along with a share of Norway. Under Eirik she was for many years a symbol of Viking prowess. Two hundred years later in the 13th Century, when the chronicler Snorri Sturluson recorded King Olaf's saga, the *Long Serpent*'s oaken bones were still visible beside Trondheim Fjord, a reminder of the greatness of the Viking mariner and the boldness of the Viking warrior.

Both fact and myth play honored roles in this 12-foot-high picture stone, one of hundreds of towering limestone memorials raised in honor of fallen Viking warriors on the Swedish island of Gotland. The stone's upper panels depict, from the top, a fierce battle, the fallen hero borne to burial atop a steed, and finally his triumphant entrance into Valhalla. The Viking ship at bottom may symbolize the passage of the soul.

A battle of dragon ship against dragon ship

Swooping out of the dark sea mists, the Viking marauders appeared to their landbound victims as agents of a single vast and fell northern horde. But as often as the Norsemen set upon alien peoples, they fought at home among themselves in an endless series of fratricidal wars. It was during these battles that the Norsemen conducted what were probably the first great naval engagements in the history of northern Europe.

The first sea battle of major proportions took place at Hafrsfjord in southwestern Norway sometime around the year 885 when Harald Fairhair, according to a saga, "set his ships on the water, gathering people from every district" to defeat a fleet mustered by seven rebellious nobles, and thus secured his crown. Sea power again proved decisive in the year 1062 when Norway's Harald Hardradi fought Denmark's King Svein Estridsson in one of the greatest of all recorded Viking sea battles.

A saga relates that Svein commanded 300 ships at Nissa, a river in western Sweden, and sent them against only 150 longships whose warriors swore fealty to Harald. But in a fight that lasted through the night, Harald's men were victorious, and the saga records that "there were more than 70 of King Svein's ships left behind"—meaning, presumably, that they were either sunk or captured.

The Vikings usually fought in placid coastal waters or fjords, where rough weather would not complicate the fray. The defenders customarily lashed their longships gunwale to gunwale with the largest ships in the center, leaving only a few small ships free to ferry fresh troops along the line and carry off the wounded. The storm of arrows, wrote one saga writer, made "the sea look as it does in heavy rain in still weather." When the vessels were locked in combat, the king or ranking earl directed the soldiers from the stern, surrounded by a protective wall of armed shieldmen. Battling with swords, spears and axes, the Norsemen methodically hacked away at one another until either the attackers fled in their ships or the defenders gathered around their lord to seek a glorious death.

Rounding the precipitous headlands of a fjord, a fleet of Viking attackers (background) begins to drop sail and row into combat as their rivals hastily maneuver their own longships into a battle line. While one crew of defenders unsteps a mast to clear for action (far right), others are swinging their ships into line (center) and lashing the vessels together to form a floating bulwark. A small eight-oared craft (foreground, right) ferries additional men to a longship and off-loads unnecessary equipment in order to clear the larger vessel's deck for action. Ashore, the smoke of smouldering signal fires still summons tardy defenders to arms.

A crosshatch of arrows and spears fills the sky as the first attacking longship drives into the center of the defenders' line. At left a pikeman rears back to hurl his weapon while a comrade nearby stands ready to send a heavy stone crashing into the enemy ranks. In the bow the invaders crowd forward, using their shields to fend off the blows of the defenders, who include at right a shrieking, bare-headed berserker wielding a gigantic battle-ax. Meanwhile an attacker, oblivious to the mounting casualties lying on the deck of his ship, swings a four-pronged grappling hook in order to bind his vessel more securely to the enemy.

RICHARD SCHLECHT

Having cut loose from formation in an attempt to flee, one of the defenders' vessels is rammed amidships, its stout oars snapping off like kindling under the impact of the enemy prow. Nearby, another vessel—already holed and swamped by the attackers—spills its surviving crew members into the icy water, where they fall easy prey to one of the attackers' mop-up crews. At lower right, defenders are swept from the decks of an isolated longship, slaughtered mercilessly and pitched over the sides as the triumphant invaders, assisted by a crew of reinforcements in a small ship (far right), take possession of their new prize.

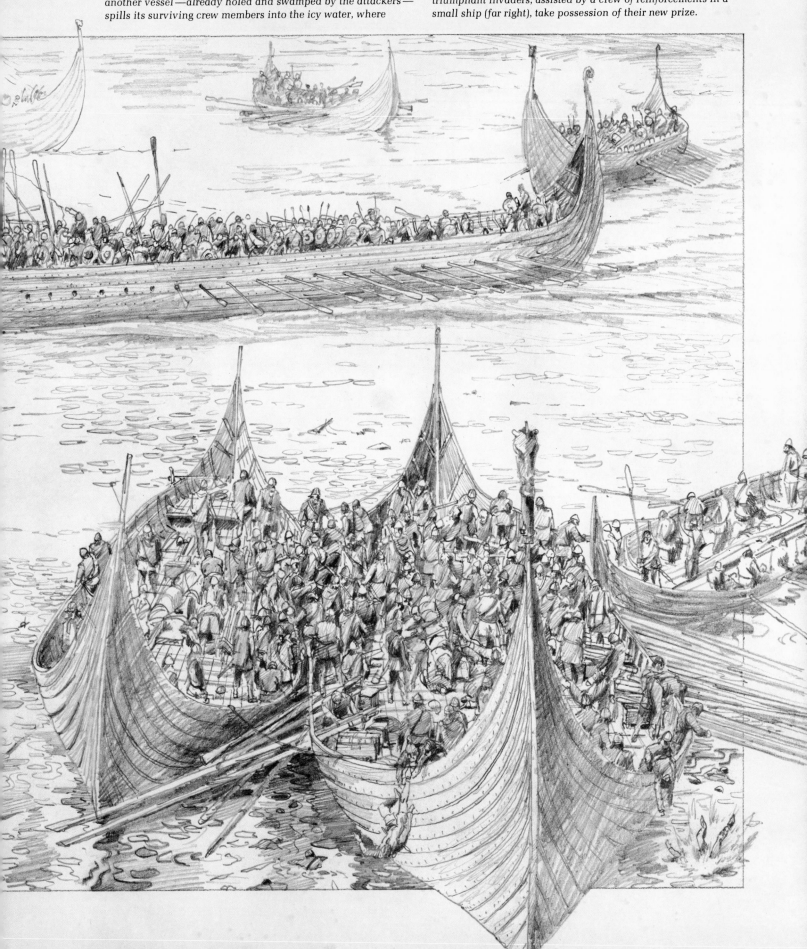

Raiders turned to rulers and nation builders

n the month of November 885, an immense fleet of 700 Viking vessels—one of the largest naval assemblages of the entire warrior age—sailed up the River Seine, penetrating into the very heart of France. At its head were Sigfred and Orm, two Viking chieftains who had been raiding in Frankish lands throughout the decade. On and on they led their fleet, pillaging as they went, until on the 26th day of that bleak month they were 100 miles inland and before the walled city of Paris—then concentrated on the boat-shaped Ile de la Cité in the middle of the river, and already crowned with a cathedral and holding command of the Seine and waterways beyond. From this all-important island city, two fortified bridges arched over the river, one reaching to either bank. The Vikings could proceed no farther without taking them.

The ruler of Paris, Charles the Fat, a great-grandson of Charlemagne and nominal head of the dwindled Frankish empire, was preoccupied elsewhere with fractious cousins trying to secede from the empire. All that remained to guard the bridges were 200 Parisian knights and their men-at-arms under Count Odo, marquis of the province of Neustria, and Bishop Joscelin, the city's ranking clergyman.

Against this scanty defense, thousands upon thousands of ship-borne warriors hurled themselves into action. "Horrible spectacle!" exclaimed the monk Abbo, who witnessed the event from inside the cathedral precincts. In moments the air was a blizzard of arrows; the stones of the fortress towers resounded with the clang of thousands of spears hurled against them, and after the Vikings flung flaming torches at the battlements the whole city was ablaze with flames that painted the sky "the color of copper," as Abbo put it.

Yet at day's end, the ruined island city was still miraculously in the hands of its brave defenders. The Viking assault subsided—only to be renewed three days later. Then day after day, week after week, the Vikings pummeled Paris, while Count Odo and Bishop Joscelin and their handful of stalwarts clung tenaciously to the walls of their city.

For all the ferocity of the attack, the Vikings did not succeed in taking Paris. But they did invest both banks of the river, and from there they held the city under siege for the better part of a year, simultaneously ravaging the French countryside for miles around. Not until late in 886 did Charles the Fat bring tardy relief to the embattled Parisians, who by now were facing famine and pestilence. And then his action was that of a craven, victim of blackmail. Instead of fighting off the Vikings, he granted them safe passage up the Seine—flouting the heroism of the Parisians—and in addition paid the warriors 700 pounds of silver to go and harass his rebellious subjects in Burgundy.

The long siege of Paris and its stunning aftermath exemplified how great Viking might and Viking ambitions had grown since the first few shiploads of warriors had descended howling upon England's Lindisfarne monastary less than a century before. Those early summertime hit-and-run raids were but the merest of larcenies compared with what the Norsemen learned to visit on the lands of northwestern Europe. As shrewd and pragmatic as they were violent, they soon saw the wasteful folly of returning home to Scandinavia, or even to the Shetland or Ork-

By the 11th Century, when this tiny statuette of a block-jawed warrior one and a half inches high was made from an elk horn by a Norse craftsman, the Vikings controlled northern Europe's coastal regions, including wide areas of France and most of the British Isles. Wrote an agonized Irish chronicler: "The sea spewed forth floods of foreigners, so that no haven, no landing place, no stronghold, no fort, no castle might be found, but it was submerged by waves of Vikings."

ney Islands, after each raid. Instead, growing numbers of Vikings established quarters in easily defended islands in the mouths of major rivers that led inland from the sea, and used them as bases for their murderous forays all year round.

Finding the country and the clime to their liking, these Vikings took to remaining as unwelcome guests for longer and longer periods of time. And now, in the last quarter of the Ninth Century, they were swarming out of their longships in an ever-growing host, and seeking not simply to plunder but to conquer and carve out vast territories to rule.

The massive Viking invasions of France, and of England and Ireland as well, opened a new and fascinating chapter in the era of the Norsemen. The nature and history of the beset lands, the traditions and bent of their peoples, and the strengths and weaknesses of the various Viking leaders made each of these three invasions very different from the others. And each produced a different—and sometimes surprising—result. In sum, they altered forever the course of medieval history.

Navigating their longships up the River Seine, a horde of ladder-carrying Vikings takes Paris by surprise during an early raid in the year 845. The city's stout defenses, as seen in an imaginative 19th Century French rendering, stalemated the Vikings on more than one occasion.

Nowhere did the Vikings reach deeper, plunder with richer rewards or settle more effectively than in the vast inchoate empire once ruled by Charlemagne. When Charlemagne died in 814, he left an immense inheritance that reached from the Atlantic coast of France east to modern Hungary and from the North Sea south to the Mediterranean. All this went to his son Louis the Pious, so called for his earnest devotion to Christianity; in 823 Louis dispatched missionaries to Denmark in an early attempt to Christianize the pagan Vikings in their homeland. But he paid too little attention to the affairs of his secular state—and to his own household. When he died he left three quarrelsome sons—Charles the Bald, Louis the German and Lothar, who for some reason seems to have escaped an epithet. These brothers went to war among themselves, which tore the empire asunder. Lothar retained the title of emperor and roughly the lands that are today Frisia, Provence, Burgundy and Lombardy. Charles the Bald got the remainder of what is modern France, while Louis the German got the lands roughly equivalent to modern Germany, which accounts for his name. And all three acquired packs of wolfish nobles as eager for plunder as the Vikings themselves. Naturally, the Vikings found this great and anarchic mass irresistible.

Typical of a number of brief alliances and rapid conquests made by the Norsemen was an incident that occurred in June of 842 along the River Loire, where an ambitious nobleman named Count Lambert was leading a raggle-taggle army in rebellion against Charles the Bald. The count had been trying without success to seize Nantes, an old Roman-walled city that fronted on the river and commanded the province of Brittany. But his men could not breach the walls, and they had no means of attacking from the riverside—until the Vikings arrived in the area.

The Norsemen, in an expedition of 67 longships, had sailed out into the Atlantic and down the west coast of France to the estuary of the Loire. There they stopped, confronted by a bewildering maze of shallow channels meandering among brush-choked islands for 100 miles upstream. They were apparently encamped, wondering what to do, when an emissary from Count Lambert arrived with a proposition. The worthy count seems to have seen the Vikings as the answer to his prayers, and offered to pilot them upstream to places of plunder in exchange for their aid in capturing the city of Nantes. The Vikings, always eager to seize any expedient that suited their purposes, readily agreed.

The date chosen for the joint attack was June 23—and a cunning choice it was. June 23 was St. John's Eve, the shortest night of the year and one marked since prehistoric times in Europe by bonfires and fertility rites welcoming in the summer. For that reason the people of Nantes were too preoccupied with celebrating to notice what was happening on the river. The boats of the Vikings glided silently to a halt on the banks of the Loire at Nantes. There, with guttural roars that were by now all too familiar along the coastlines of Europe, the warriors stormed into the merrymaking crowds, slaying left and right, and setting the tower afire.

Count Lambert, having wrested Nantes from Charles the Bald, then disappeared from history. Clearly, he gave the city no relief from the Vikings, who were to raid it in the future as they chose.

As for the immediate Vikings, after a few days they retired to the mouth of the Loire with all their booty. Then, instead of returning to Scandinavia, they settled on the large island of Noirmoutier just south of the Loire, and from that depot they scoured the countryside on both sides of the river, destroying towns, pirating merchant pack trains and robbing farmers of their cattle and produce. "The number of ships increases, the endless flood of Vikings never ceases to grow bigger," wrote the scholar Ermentarius about these years in the 840s. "Everywhere Christ's people are the victims of massacre, burning and plunder. The Vikings overrun all that lies before them, and none can withstand them. They seize Bordeaux, Périgueux, Limoges, Angoulême, Toulouse. Angers, Tours and Orléans are made deserts. Ships past counting voyage up the Seine, and throughout the entire region evil grows strong."

Charles the Fat's expedient in 886 of paying the Vikings off in silver— such tribute came to be known as Danegeld, or "Danish money"—was neither the first nor the last futile attempt to encourage the Vikings to depart by making them rich. Between 845 and 926 the French kings taxed their people unconscionably to make 13 payments to the Vikings totaling more than 43,000 pounds of silver and 685 pounds of gold. And still the plunderers came back. So frequent were their visits that little was left of cities like Rouen, Nantes and Orléans, which from their locations on the Seine and the Loire had served as marketplaces for the hinterland. The noblemen either fell in battle or fled from the marauders. The monks all fled from their abbeys, and great monasteries like Jumièges, which had kept alive a flickering flame of culture after the barbarian triumph over Rome, were now only roofless, windowless walls.

But sometime at the end of the 9th Century or the beginning of the 10th, there arose a Viking leader of extraordinary prowess and sagacity who shaped an entirely new destiny for the Vikings. His name was Hrolf, and he must have been an extremely large man: he was nicknamed Gongu-Hrolf, Hrolf the Walker, because no horse could carry him. A plausible legend has it that he was a Norwegian, scion of a family that had fled as outlaws from Norway to northern Scotland to seek freedom and fortune there. From that land's fog-shrouded, cliff-girt coast with its narrow, rock-bound inlets, Hrolf took part in many raids, going sometimes to the coast of England, other times to that of France. By the early part of the 10th Century he and his followers had apparently overrun and occupied part of the old Roman province of Neustria on the Seine.

It was a place worth having, rich with orchards and lush meadows that must have looked like paradise to a man raised in the grim North. And Hrolf was evidently interested in more than loot, for he stayed on.

After many years that are veiled in darkness, the light of history flashes on for a brief moment in the year 911. At that time Hrolf, his name by now changed to Rollo, reached an agreement with the Frankish king. He was another Charles, grandson of Charles the Bald, who had fought his brothers for the empire and won the lion's share of France. This Charles, a youth in whom the blood of Charlemagne ran so thin that his subjects derisively called him Charles the Simple, was induced to sign a formal treaty with Rollo at St. Clair-sur-Epte, on a small river running into the Seine between Paris and Rouen.

By the terms of the treaty, Charles formally agreed to cede to Rollo what the Viking had already more or less taken — the broad valley of the lower Seine, soon to be called Normandy after the Norsemen. With it went the title of Count of Rouen, a designation Rollo's descendants would magnify into Duke of Normandy as they expanded their holdings to a broad swath on the northwest shoulder of France, about 175 miles by 60 and bounded by the important market towns of Evreux, Chartres, St. Lo and Bayeux. In return, Rollo was to swear fealty to the King, to look to the defense of his own domain and to be baptized a Christian and uphold the faith of the realm.

It is not difficult to imagine the contrast when these two ill-matched leaders met — Rollo, the roistering giant of a Viking sea lord, his huge frame jangling with golden arm rings and amulets stamped with the hammer of Thor; Charles, elegant in linen shirt and breeches and a cloak decorated in silk, his head perhaps buzzing with illusions of imperial grandeur but no doubt haunted by fears of rebellion.

Despite their differences, both men recognized that they had certain goals that were reconciled by the treaty. Charles the Simple had the not-so-simple task of holding down more than a dozen fractious nobles in his own realm and dealing with repeated raids from the Vikings as well; Rollo wanted land to rule. The treaty served them both. For Rollo it made legitimate his presence in Normandy; for Charles it provided a buffer between his harassed kingdom and new Viking arrivals from the sea.

Rollo could be a brutal man. According to one tradition, when some peasants sought the right to hunt and fish in Rollo's woods, lakes and rivers, he dispatched his uncle, Count Rudolph, to cut off a hand and a foot of each of the would-be poachers. But he was also sharp-witted and practical. He let himself be baptized, and he lost no time in restoring the churches that he and his fellow Vikings had sacked. His new-found Christianity probably did not greatly affect his personal beliefs one way or another. It was later recounted that when he was on his deathbed he asked to be buried in the cathedral of Rouen and he ordered large sums of gold to be given to Christian churches; he also called for human sacrifices to be made to the pagan gods. Presumably, then, whether St. Peter or Thor met him in the hereafter, he would be assured of a welcome.

The immediate temporal benefit from his conversion was political. He won the churchmen, who alone could read and write, over to his side, and by showing favor to the Church he got religious scholars and scribes to work for his interests — which were nothing less than the establishment of a workable state.

Settling himself at Rouen overlooking the Seine, Rollo kept his bargain with Charles the Simple; there were no further Viking raids upriver into Charles's realm. Though he handed out parcels of land to his followers, he kept power tightly centralized in his own hands — belying an old tale his Vikings loved to tell about their first entry into Normandy: how when an officer of Charles the Simple shouted across a stream at the advancing Viking band, asking who their leader was, the cry came back, "We know no masters. All of us are equals."

Power was firmly arranged in a pyramid, with Rollo unchallenged at the top. In times of emergency he supplied Charles with men-at-arms, and Viking men-at-arms were murderous fighters. At harvesttime each

The august monarch Charlemagne, King of the Franks and Emperor of the West, carries an orb as a symbol of earthly power in this Ninth Century equestrian bronze. During his reign as emperor, from 800 to 814, the Norsemen tore savagely at the northern fringes of his empire in what is now Holland and Germany, prompting him to order the building of a large navy and to negotiate the first written peace treaty between the Vikings and a Christian king.

year, those same men-at-arms supplied a percentage of the land's yield to Rollo, just as they supplied military service at his bidding.

Normandy as founded by Rollo was to become in only a few generations the most formidable state that Europe had seen since the fall of Rome 500 years before, and the model of the medieval fiefdom.

As Rollo and his fellow Vikings put down roots in Normandy, they inevitably loosened their ties with their Scandinavian homeland. The Old Norse language was quick to go. The first wave of invaders had come over with few if any women; when they settled down they took French wives and concubines. The children grew up speaking their mothers' tongue. Only a generation later, according to the chronicles, when Rollo's son Duke William Longsword wanted his own son to learn the ancestral language, no one in Rouen could teach it. He had to send the boy almost 100 miles away to Bayeux, which had the most recent arrivals from Scandinavia and therefore some speakers of Old Norse.

Rollo sired an extraordinary family. He was succeeded through six generations by descendants who shared his qualities of sharp wit, practicality, leadership and administrative skill. It was a sixth-generation direct descendant of Rollo's, Duke William of Normandy, who achieved the greatest feat of arms in many an age—the conquest of all England, a strongly Viking England, in one blow in 1066 (pages 162-169).

As in France, the Viking presence in England had evolved through an endless series of raids, incursions and devastations into invasions on a grand scale. Under the weight of the Viking assault, the petty kingdoms of Northumbria, East Anglia and Mercia collapsed one by one, their strength drained, their royal lineages extinguished. By 880 only one Anglo-Saxon kingdom survived, Wessex in the southwest. And even that might have succumbed had it not been for the firm hand and cool head of the young King Alfred who ruled there. He was the only English monarch to receive the epithet "the Great," and he deserved it.

Alfred dealt with the Vikings on two levels—one political, the other military. It was obvious that the Vikings had overrun the lands to the north and east, and Alfred was enough of a pragmatist to accept that fact and seek to make it work for him. He therefore drew up a treaty, which he signed with the Danish leader Guthrum, acknowledging the Viking claim to the conquered lands. Alfred, as the sole remaining Anglo-Saxon monarch of any stature, was signifying his people's intent to live in peace, if possible, with the invaders. And he hoped to encourage them to work the land instead of incessantly trying to destroy it—and him.

But Alfred also knew that treaties gain force and acceptance only from the strength that backs them up. And so he set out to make Wessex wellnigh impregnable. First, he revamped the levy system for fighting men. "The King," says the Anglo-Saxon Chronicle, "divided his levies into two sections, so that there was always half at home and half on active service." Under the new arrangement, men could be on their farms with their families half the time—and hence were less inclined to desert.

Next he built a series of fortified enclosures into which the peasants could drive their cattle and take refuge themselves when Viking invaders appeared. Soon the Vikings were appearing less frequently in Wessex, for on the banks of the River Lea Alfred placed two forts that impeded an invader's passage down the river.

Finally, and most important, Alfred was the only ruler in all Europe to deal the Vikings a blow with their own mightiest weapon—the warship. Sometime in the 890s he ordered the building of a fleet. Alfred's ships were "almost twice as long" as the Viking ships, relates the Chronicle. "Some had 60 oars, some more." They were designed by the King himself, not on the Danish model, but, says the Chronicle, "as it seemed to the King they might be most serviceable."

The Chronicle calls them swifter than the Viking longships, which is unlikely. But they were higher and more difficult for the enemy to board, and as coastal defense vessels they were also probably heavier and steadier, with flat, bargelike bottoms that drew even less water than the Viking ships. In any event, they seem to have been remarkably effective. In one skirmish in 896, noted the Chronicle, Alfred's ships caught six Viking vessels stranded at low tide in a southern port. Alfred's men overcame four of the ships and killed most of the crewmen. Two vessels managed to get away. But during the year, relates the Chronicle, 20 Viking vessels, "men and all, perished along the south coast."

Before he died in 899, Alfred alone in England had managed to stalemate the Vikings in combat. But more important, perhaps, the treaty he had signed in 886 with the Danish leader Guthrum appears to have had some of the calming effect Alfred desired. Instead of regarding the lands to the north as alien territory, the Vikings began to think of them as their own, to settle them, to meld with the Anglo-Saxon inhabitants and to enrich them with the culture of their native Denmark.

This Viking sector of England comprised about 25,000 square miles and was bounded in the south by a line running diagonally northwest from just beyond London to Chester on the Irish Sea, and in the north by a line running from the mouth of the River Tees to the North Channel of the Irish Sea. And so Danish did it become that it was known as the Danelaw, since the laws and customs of Denmark obtained there.

How many Danes crossed the North Sea to settle as farmers and traders in the Danelaw is a question much debated by scholars. Some think that they formed only a thin layer of military aristocrats who ousted English landlords from their property but did not otherwise occupy the land in any numbers. Other scholars believe that there was a massive migration from Denmark throughout the 9th and 10th Centuries. They have two good reasons for thinking so. The most convincing is the fact that instead of losing their language, as did the Vikings who began to speak French in Normandy, the Danes had a powerful influence on the English language: linguistically, they led, rather than followed, the local culture.

There are hundreds of place names in England ending in the suffix -by, from the Old Norse meaning farm or village: Derby, Whitby, Grimsby, and so on. Even more pervasive are the thousands of Norse-derived words in the everyday English vocabulary. The modern Danish philologist Otto Jespersen once noted that "an Englishman cannot *thrive* or be *ill* or *die* without Scandinavian words; they are to the language what *bread* and *eggs* are to the daily fare." The list goes on and on: *take, call, window, husband, sky, anger, low, scant, loose, ugly, wrong, happy.* In

Enfeebled by the relentless Viking incursions and the rising power of feudal barons, Charlemagne's grandson Charles the Bald—here enthroned at court with tresses that belie his name—was reduced to bribing the Norse marauders with vast amounts of silver in the futile hope that they would spare his empire and concentrate their attacks elsewhere.

Frocked in ecclesiastical vestments, Bishop Froncon of Rouen surrenders the town to the triumphant pagan Viking leader Hrolf in this illustration from a 15th Century French manuscript recounting the conquest of Normandy by the Danes in 911. The artist chose to depict the conquerors in heavy armor, but in fact the Vikings would not have worn such cumbersome gear, favoring speed and agility over safety in combat.

the opinion of numerous scholars, so many and such fundamental words could not have been brought in by an army; they had to have come on the tongues of Danish mothers and children—and, of course, farmers, merchants and craftsmen.

In addition to their language, the Danes brought laws and the means for enforcing them. In Scandinavia they had kept the laws by oral tradition; here they committed them to writing. A code for the year 997 in the Danelaw provides for courts consisting of 12 leading men—called thanes—to take an oath on sacred relics that they would neither accuse the innocent nor shield the guilty. "Let the judgment stand on which the thanes are agreed," says the code; "if they differ let that stand which eight of them have pronounced." Here is the first assertion in English law of majority rule, and the first provision for trial by jury.

Whether they came as an army or as a migration, the Vikings did not massacre or drive away the native population. The two peoples lived side by side and sooner or later began consorting together—albeit not without some blue-nosed English expressions of indignation. A contemporary chronicler, John of Wallingford, complained sourly that the

Danes were always combing their hair, changing their underwear and taking baths on Saturday "in order to overcome the chastity of the English women and procure the daughters of noblemen as their mistresses."

But while the Danes and the English may have learned to live together more or less in peace, the Danelaw did not become a truly stable and efficient state on the Norman model. The Danish settlers never managed to throw up a leader of Rollo's stature who was equal to the task of unifying the country and enforcing their democratically conceived laws. Instead, the Danes consumed much of their energy in waging petty feuds among themselves or in beating off incursions from their ambitious Viking cousins in Norway and elsewhere. And as the years wore on, some Danish chieftains again cast covetous eyes on the south and resumed their raiding across the border from the Danelaw.

Well they might, for southern England was growing weak and vulnerable. Throughout the realm made safe by Alfred the Great a century before, the fabric of government was rapidly unraveling. In 978 one of the most worthless kings in all of English history acceded to the throne. He was Ethelred, aptly nicknamed "the Unready," who inherited the Crown at the unripe age of 12 and for the rest of his life was benighted with personal indecision and poor counselors. In that sorry state, as the 10th Century drew to a close, all England—not only Ethelred's realm, but also the partially materialized Danelaw—was to face a great threat from the Vikings across the North Sea.

In Scandinavia two leaders of note were securing their own realms—the Norwegian Olaf Tryggvason, descended from Harald Fairhair and in his own right a formidable warrior who went into battle resplendent in a scarlet cloak, and the Dane Svein Forkbeard. Both now turned their might abroad—not as freebooters but as kings bent on conquest.

The first attacks of the new Viking wave came in 991, when Norway's Olaf sailed to southern England with a fleet of 93 ships. In quick succession Olaf's warriors ravaged the ports of Folkestone and Sandwich. Next they landed within 30 miles of London, near the town of Maldon, on an island with a causeway leading to the mainland. There an English leader named Byrhtnoth valiantly attempted to halt the Vikings. But he and his men were overwhelmed—and the whole of southeastern England lay open to the invaders.

The unready Ethelred's response to this threat was to try unwisely to buy Olaf off with a payment of 10,000 pounds of silver—coins, brooches, arm rings, torques and ingots wrung from his unhappy subjects, together with food and drink for the lusty Viking army.

That expedient was the first of many that succeeded only in enraging Ethelred's Anglo-Saxon subjects. This time, the payment brought them surcease from the Viking harassment—but only for three years. In 994 the Norwegian Olaf was back, this time allied with the Danish Svein Forkbeard. After collecting 16,000 pounds of silver, the two kings returned to Scandinavia. But not for long. Svein was soon to return and to embark on a campaign that would take him the length and breadth of England and occupy him for more than a decade.

He began in the southeast corner of Wessex. For the year 999 the

Chronicle recounts how "the host again came round into the Thames." This time, at long last, Ethelred gathered his courage and attempted to fight the invaders. What is more, he thought to make a major stand. "The King with his counselors," relates the Chronicle, "decided to advance against them with both naval and land forces." But unfortunately for the feckless Ethelred, nothing went right. Delay followed delay, and neither the ships nor the soldiers ever saw combat. "So in the end," advises the Chronicle, "these preparations were a complete failure. They effected nothing except the oppression of the people and the waste of money." The Chronicle for 999 ends on that unhappy note, without recording the tribute exacted by the Danes, but it must have been great.

In 1001 the Danes returned again, and after another year's harassment Ethelred yielded once more, this time paying Svein 24,000 pounds of silver. Then Ethelred spitefully gave orders for "all the Danish people who were in the land to be slain on St. Brice's Day," November 13. Here was a mindless atrocity, for there was considerable commerce between the English and the Danes, and numbers of Danes had settled peacefully in the south. How many were rounded up and butchered is not known. But the mass murders infuriated the Danish King Svein, and for more reasons than one. Among those killed was his sister Gunnhild.

Svein had the means to retaliate, for he had been assembling a great force. Four extraordinary military camps were scattered about the perimeter of Denmark, all of them on navigable waters leading to the sea. They were carefully planned compounds, each with a number of boat-shaped barracks built of wood for 60 to 75 men, presumably warship crews, and each camp with a stout defensive palisade around the perimeter. Together the camps could quarter at least 4,000 warriors at a time. It was from these camps that Svein now launched a series of attacks on England with which the misbegotten Ethelred was quite unable to cope.

Though the English king mustered a warship from every 300 hides of his realm (a hide was a geographical unit representing about 120 arable acres), he could not control his fleet. In a battle off Sandwich in 1009, the Vikings burned 80 of his vessels. Another 20 defected to the enemy, and Ethelred, said the Chronicle simply, "went home"—meaning that he deserted his forces and fled to his nearest redoubt.

The Danes anchored their ships in Sandwich on August 1 of that year, went ashore, and looted Ethelred's kingdom far and wide, collecting 36,000 pounds of silver. By the following summer the Danes were everywhere. "When the enemy was in the east, then our levies were mustering in the west, and when they were in the south, then our levies were in the north," says the 1010 Chronicle ruefully. "In the end there was no leader who was willing to raise levies, but each fled as quickly as he could."

That same year, Norwegian Vikings, under yet another Olaf, this one surnamed Haraldsson, sailed up the Thames and tore down London Bridge with grappling hooks, inspiring the rhyme that is sung in nurseries to this day. A year later, in the autumn of 1011, the Danish Vikings of King Svein reached Canterbury and seized, among other prisoners, the elderly archbishop, whom they pelted with stones and the severed heads of cattle before crushing his skull with an ax.

Throughout this decade that had been so tumultuous for the south of

Alfred the Great of Wessex is pictured with a crown and scepter in an illumination from a 13th Century manuscript recounting his victory over the Danes in 878. The object below—of crystal and gold with an enameled portrait of a figure bearing crossed scepters—is reputed to be part of King Alfred's own royal scepter.

England, the Danelaw had been exempt from Svein's attacks. But in the summer of 1013 he drew it into the fray. Advancing to York and Northumbria, he secured allies from among the Danish chieftains there, and then turned south to deliver a final crushing assault. In quick succession Oxford, Winchester, Bath and London fell. Ethelred fled for his life to Normandy, and Svein installed himself as king of all England.

Only five weeks later the conquering Svein was dead at the age of 55, whether of sickness or of accident the records do not say. In Denmark he left an heir—his son Knut—who, though a stripling only 18 years old, was equal to the task of carrying on where his father had left off.

In 1015 Knut sailed from Scandinavia with 200 ships to claim his father's legacy. He first crushed the straggling remains of Ethelred's army and then put to rout another force raised by Ethelred's son Edmund. Knut next levied the highest single Danegeld in history—82,000 pounds of silver from throughout the realm, of which 10,000 came from London alone. Then, instead of making off with the loot, he used it to pay off his troops and demobilize much of his army.

Some of the Vikings went home to Scandinavia, but many others settled down to reside in the new realm they had conquered—chief among them Knut, who ruled as king.

A saga says of Knut that his nose, "which was long, narrow and slightly bent, somewhat marred his good looks." And he had a full share of wild Viking blood in his veins; in a fit of rage over a chess game, according to legend, he ordered a minion to kill his faithful friend and brother-in-law, Earl Ulf. Nevertheless, he was in most respects a temperate, farseeing and realistic monarch. When his courtiers, bedazzled by his triumphs, told him he could make the tides stand still, he sat on his throne by the seaside, with the waves washing around him, to show them that he was human.

This Danish Viking gave England its first peace in a quarter century. Since Christianity was the religion of a majority of his subjects, he himself submitted to baptism. He restored monasteries and consecrated churches. And in a written code of law, the first to apply to all England, he proclaimed Christianity the faith of the land and required the populace to support the Church with silver and crops.

The secular portions of Knut's law spelled out, among other things, what may have been Western Europe's first written inheritance tax. A certain percentage of the estate of an earl went on his death to the king; lower-ranking nobles paid proportionately less. Other taxes were raised annually to defend the realm and pay for professional soldiers and seamen; some 3,000 pounds, for example, was collected annually to pay the wages of the seamen on Knut's warships. These taxes were no doubt an annoyance, like taxes everywhere, but still they offered a merciful release from the extortionate Danegelds of yore.

When he died quietly in his bed in 1035 at the age of 39 or 40, Knut left an England united and prosperous, and content to be under Viking rule. It seemed that the Norsemen's conquest was complete.

But Knut's sons proved not to be of their father's stature. They fought constantly among themselves—like the Vikings of the past—and succeeded only in losing the Crown of England to a son of Ethelred's, Edward the Confessor. He in turn—refusing, out of excessive piety, to sleep with his wife—produced no heirs at all. He thus guaranteed a scramble for succession, which led in 1066 to the Norman invasion that spelled the doom of the Viking era in England.

Scarcely 60 miles west of England, across a shallow sea, lay another somewhat smaller island, fertile and well watered, and an early object of Viking attentions. This was Ireland. It was a country of contrasts, enormously rich in some things, abysmally poor in others, virtually leaderless yet indomitable, the easiest prey of all but in the end the victim that most frustrated the Norsemen. For the Vikings, despite all their force of arms, encountered qualities of canniness and resilience in the Irish that they found both befuddling and exhausting. They never did conquer Ireland in the sense that they subjugated England or carved a state for themselves in France. Indeed, after the climactic Battle of Clontarf in 1014, the Irish could claim with some justice to have been the first to have thrust the Vikings back to the shores whence they had come.

When the Vikings arrived on the island around 800, Ireland had the most intellectually advanced culture of the West. Its lush hills were crowned with uncounted monasteries; the bell towers of nearly 100 such institutions survived as late as the 19th Century, and no one knows how many more succumbed to the ravages of war and weather. These centers of study delved into all manner of subjects, from astronomy to theology, and contributed to the learning of England and the Continent; it was to Irish monks that Charlemagne turned when he founded a school at the Frankish court, and from Irish script and illumination that the exquisitely crafted Carolingian volumes of his descendants derived.

But for all the monks' erudition, the great mass of the Irish were lamentably behind in affairs of this world. Economically, Ireland had no commerce more sophisticated than barter. Technologically, the Irish had no ships worthy of the name, only hide-covered fishing craft, and their weapons were inferior. The Viking invaders, says an old Irish poem, wrought havoc "because of the excellence of their polished, ample, treble, heavy, trusty, glittering corselets; their hard, strong, valiant swords; and their well-riveted long spears."

Politically, the Irish had been living in virtual isolation since the beginning of history. They had not been visited by the Roman legions that had swept over Continental Europe and England in the First Century, B.C., and so they had not even the primordial vestiges of the legal codes and administrative practices that helped to forge the *modus vivendi* between Vikings and natives in England and France.

Neither had they any experience in putting aside petty quarrels long enough to sustain a common cause against a common danger. Their only hierarchy was a kaleidoscopic collection of rival petty kings whose ancient jealousies and quick tempers kept them at odds with one another and with the nominal high king who reigned at Tara, about 20 miles from the eastern coast. "Alas," mourned one early chronicler, "it is pitiful for the Irish to continue the evil habit of fighting amongst themselves and that they do not rise together against the Norwegians."

Throughout the seven sparsely settled provinces of Ireland—Con-

Secrets of the Vikings' wizardry in wood

Most modern ships are built from the inside out, with a more or less rigid skeleton of ribs to which an outer skin of planks or plates is attached. This offers strength at the expense of weight. The Vikings, however, built their ships from the outside in, first forming a thin shell of oak planks and then adding ribs for strength. This gave them a light yet supple and seaworthy craft that seemed to skim the very tops of the waves instead of plowing heavily through them.

The secret of Viking success was superb craftsmanship. Their shipwrights paid great attention to the way each plank was cut, and to what thickness. Though saws were known in those times, the Vikings preferred axes, and their skill with a blade approached genius. To preserve the maximum strength of the wood, every tree was split lengthwise into a number of segments, each one running from bark to core; the shipwrights then adzed these triangular segments into uniform planks of the proper length and thickness.

On an average vessel there would be 16 such planks on each side of the hull. They would range in thickness from one inch below the water line to 1¾ inches at the water line, and slimming to ½ inch at the gunwale. Even the thickest of

the planks was thin enough to be bent by hand into the necessary compound curves and affixed to the huge stempost and sternpost; no steam bending was necessary. Working up from the keel, the Vikings joined each plank to the one below in an overlapping fashion known today as clinker, or lapstrake, construction. The planks were caulked with twisted and tarred animal hair, then fastened with roundheaded iron rivets spaced 7¼ inches apart that were driven from the outside and clenched through small iron plates on the inside. The result was a seal that would remain watertight even as the hull flexed in heavy seas.

Once the 32 planks of the hull were in place, 19 ribs formed from naturally U-shaped boughs of oak were placed in the hull. They were ingeniously lashed with flexible spruce-root bindings to knobs that had been left on the inside of each plank when it was first hewn. Crossbeams, anchored to the sides with wooden knees, spanned the hull above each rib to complete the ship's lateral reinforcement and provide a footing for the deck planks. In the center of the hull was the keelson, a massive block of oak into which the base of the mast was set. Spanning four ribs, it was

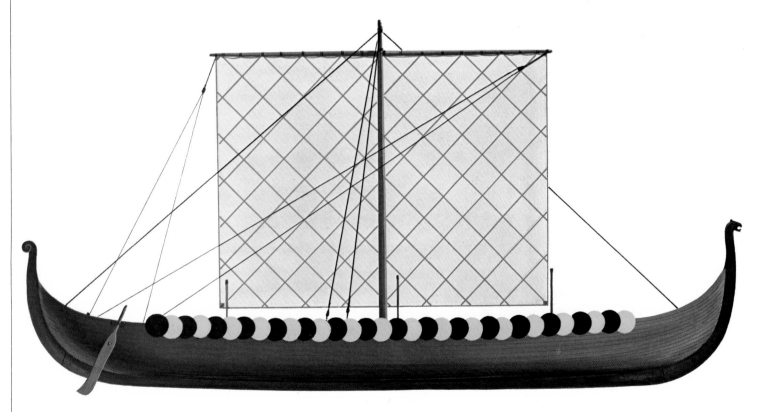

RIGGING AND SAIL OF A VIKING RAIDER

reinforced by another huge block—called the mast partner, or fish because of its piscian configuration. Three tall crutches stood along the deck from bow to stern and held the yard, sails or spars when the vessel was under oar power. On the side of the ship were attached three cleats probably used for fastening the sheet.

At the stern was the rudder, or steering oar, 10 feet high and 16 inches wide. Cut from a solid oak board, it turned on an oak block—the wart—to which it was attached by a spruce root. With typical forethought, the Vikings attached a line to a cramp near the end of the rudder blade, and thus could instantly hoist the rudder in shallow or rocky waters.

All that remained was to lay floor boards in the hull and to fashion oar holes (which would be plugged when the ship was under sail). The oars were of pine, and were made in graduated lengths from 17 to 19 feet, so that rowers in the relatively high bow would hit the water at the same time as the men seated lower amidships. At the stern a slightly raised poop was fashioned for the helmsman.

At about 75 feet in length, 15 feet in the beam and six feet from keel to gunwale, this long, low vessel weighed only 20 or so tons when fully loaded with men and equipment and drew less than three feet of water. Under sail with a following wind, she could make 11 knots and traverse close to 250 miles of ocean in a single day's run under stiff breezes. In crosswinds she could reach with the aid of tacking spars mounted on spar blocks. Even under oars she could achieve seven knots for brief periods.

When the Vikings went ashore, they could use wooden rollers to drag their treasured longship onto the beach, out of harm's way from tide or surf—or, if need be, could portage it across a neck of land and launch it on the other side.

1. STERNPOST	6. TILLER	11. KEEL	16. LASHING KNOB
2. CRAMP	7. CLEAT	12. MAST PARTNER	17. RIB
3. STEERING OAR	8. CRUTCH	13. SPAR BLOCK	18. CROSSBEAM
4. POOP DECK	9. OAR PORT	14. MAST	19. KNEE
5. WART	10. OAR-PORT SHUTTER	15. KEELSON	20. STEM

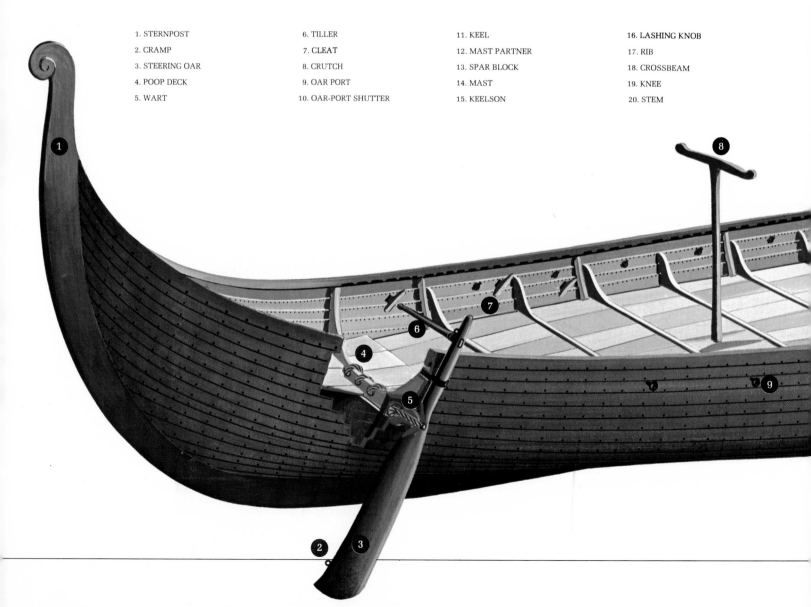

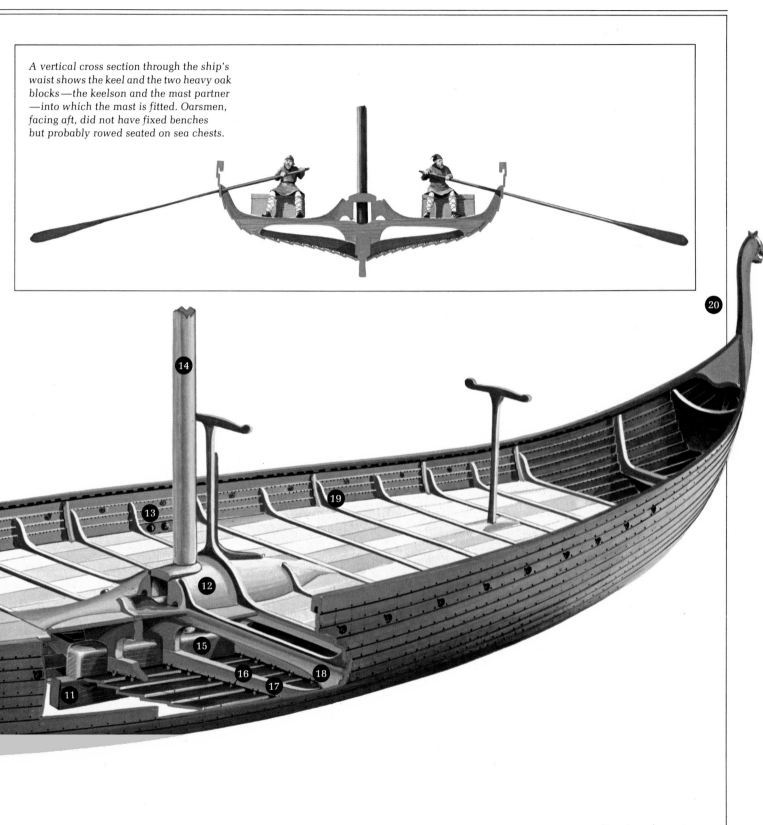

A vertical cross section through the ship's waist shows the keel and the two heavy oak blocks—the keelson and the mast partner—into which the mast is fitted. Oarsmen, facing aft, did not have fixed benches but probably rowed seated on sea chests.

John Batchelor.

naught, Munster, Leinster, Meath, Ailech, Ulaidh and Oriel—the only enemies the Irish had ever known were their neighbors, and the only strategies they employed in combat were expedients of the moment, frequently based on cunning and trickery. It was in that spirit that the Irish met the first serious Viking incursions in the 830s. And wondrous to say, that spirit of guile had its effects.

The first Viking invader of record was a Norwegian prince named Thorgils who arrived with a fleet of 120 ships carrying 10,000 warriors. He quickly seized Armagh—the ecclesiastical polestar of Ireland and the richest monastery of all. He drove out the abbot, installed himself as pagan high priest and threw up a chain of earthworks running clear to the western province of Connaught more than 100 miles away, signaling his occupation of the northern quarter of the island.

It might have seemed as though the conquest of the entire land was scarcely a battle or two away. The Irish had no Emperor Charles the Simple to bargain with the Vikings for fealty in return for a duchy, no Alfred the Great to contain the invaders behind a well-guarded border. But then, according to legend, a curious thing happened to Thorgils, something he was powerless to defend against for all his thousands of retainers. The crafty Maelsechlainn, King of Meath, sent out his daughter with 15 warriors disguised as maidens, lured Thorgils and 15 Viking captains to a lakeside tryst and drowned the lot.

However it happened, it seems certain that Thorgils met his demise. Though his death left the Vikings in Ireland without a leader, they were not without a foothold. His troops had anchored their ships in estuaries all around the Irish coast and erected wooden forts there to secure themselves. Those little forts eventually expanded up the hillsides overlooking the coasts. They were the embryos of the cities of Anagassan, Dublin, Wicklow, Wexford, Waterford, Cork and Limerick. And for the next three centuries, these cities were to be the focus of a drama that would pit not only the Vikings against the Irish, but Vikings against Vikings, and, strange to behold, Vikings and Irish against other Vikings and Irish.

Indeed, the first sizable invasion fleet to follow Thorgils' came not, as might have been expected, from fellow Norwegians bent on avenging themselves against the Irish, but from rival Danish Vikings who scented a good source of plunder in their cousins' newly established enclaves. In 849 these piratical Danes swept over the horizon in a fleet of 140 ships and fell upon the Norwegian builders of Dublin. For three years the contending Vikings waged a tug of war over the city. And the opportunistic Irish took a hand, assisting the Danes from time to time in the prayerful hope that the newcomers would oust the detested Norwegians.

But it was an alliance to make an Irishman shudder. In the aftermath of a great battle that lasted three days and three nights in 852, during which the Danes annihilated the Norwegians, messengers sent by King Maelsechlainn—he of the seductive daughter—came to the Danes' encampment to offer congratulations on the splendid victory. To their horror, the emissaries found the Danes, with perfect Viking sangfroid, cooking their food in cauldrons placed on heaps of Norwegian dead. Sparing no gory detail, an Irish chronicle describes the scene, "with spits stuck in among the corpses and the fires burning them so that their bellies

Bearing a shield emblazoned with two Viking longships, King Knut of Denmark strikes England's King Edmund with his sword in this allegorical illumination from a 13th Century manuscript. The two Kings never fought in hand-to-hand combat, but Knut's Vikings routed Edmund's forces in 1015; within a year, bemoaned the Anglo-Saxon Chronicle, Knut "succeeded to all the kingdom of England."

burst, revealing the welter of meat and pork eaten the night before."

But the Danes seem to have redeemed themselves somewhat for that barbaric performance by handing over to the Irish a chest of gold and silver coins for St. Patrick's shrine at Armagh—a deed suggesting to the chronicler that "the Danes had at least a kind of piety."

To the great pleasure of the Irish, it seemed as if the fratricidal Viking struggle might go on and on when a fresh contingent of Norwegians arrived the next year, this time under a prince known as Olaf the White. But before long the Irish had to look to their own devices. For Olaf soon routed the Danes—and then trained his lustful eye on bigger game. Gathering his forces, he launched a full-scale attack on the interior.

By now the Irish fully understood the ultimate Viking threat—absolute conquest—and they were also beginning to learn something about warfare. For the first time in the memory of Irishmen, the incumbent high king at Tara, Aed Finnlaith, managed to persuade his fellow kings to cease their interminable squabbling and rally behind him. A great army of Irish warriors was gathered, and in fury they drove the Vikings out of the countryside, inflicting terrible casualties until the Norsemen reached safety within the walls of Dublin.

And then what transpired in this wildly convoluted saga of Irish and Viking? The victorious King Aed did not lay siege to Dublin in an effort to crush the Norwegians once and for all. Instead he entered into negotiations with Olaf the White, at the end of which the King magnanimously offered Olaf the hand of no less an Irish maiden than his very own daughter. How and why this stunning romantic alliance was effected is not recorded. It may be that the King was shrewd enough to understand how fragile was his coalition of Irish clans, and wished not to fight the

Holy treasures for pagan predators

When the heathen Norsemen went a-Viking, they fell most hungrily upon the monasteries of Christian England and Ireland. For that was where the wealth of the land was gathered: gold and silver figures of saints, bishops' jewel-encrusted crosiers, exquisitely wrought reliquaries to hold the bones of saints—enough to make a Viking's avaricious heart sing, and all of it easily stripped from the virtually undefended monastic communities.

The booty was especially rich in Ireland. Christianized about 400 A.D., the Irish had 300 years of relative peace in which to nurture the arts. And since the Irish had no cities and only petty chieftains for an aristocracy, most of their precious objects were made in,

and for, their many monasteries—the closest thing they had to towns.

The Vikings learned this immediately, on their first raid at Lambay in 795, and soon, as a chronicler of the day wailed, "the ocean poured such torrents of foreigners over Erin that there was no harbor or landing place, fortress or stronghold without fleets of Vikings and pirates."

Sacking and burning one monastery after another in Ireland and England, the Vikings loaded their loot in their swift ships and took it back to Scandinavia. It is a staggering measure of Viking depredations that about one half of all the Eighth Century Irish art to survive to the present has been found in Scandinavia, mostly in Norway.

St. Matthew and a passage from the first chapter of his Gospel (below) belong to a magnificent manuscript illuminated by English monks about the year 750. This book was seized by Vikings during a Ninth Century raid but was ransomed from the raiders by one Earl Alfred. The Old English script above and below the Latin text says that Alfred and his wife "acquired this book from a heathen army" with "pure gold for the love of God."

Stolen from some unknown Irish monastery and found in Norway, this tiny, three-inch gilt-bronze figure of a saint, with its delicate, scroll-like decorations on the saint's robe and an interlaced ribbon pattern behind his head, attests to the skill attained by medieval Irish metalworkers. The now-empty eye sockets probably contained colored stones.

Expressive human faces stare from the richly decorated bronze crook of a medieval Irish crosier discovered in Helgo, Sweden. Such symbolic shepherds' crooks were prized by Viking raiders as souvenirs for their ladies at home.

Delicately interlaced bronze ribbon work decorates the wooden reliquary that a Viking took home from Ireland to Norway. The new owner's name is known because scratched in the bottom of the box are Norse runic characters that translate, "Ranvaik owns this casket."

Vikings again. Or perhaps he simply recognized the Vikings in their growing city centers as more or less permanent additions to the Irish scene, and desired to benefit his people with Viking culture and trade.

Whatever he had in mind, the alliance had welcome effects on both counts. The raids on the Irish hinterland did diminish in the second half of the Ninth Century. But even more important, Dublin, Wicklow, Wexford, Waterford and the rest were to bring the Irish their first exposure to urban life, with its amenities of flagstone streets, timbered walks and fresh water brought in conduits of hollowed tree trunks. In the Viking cities the Irish first became acquainted with the standardized weights and measures that were the basis of sophisticated trade. There they got their first taste of commerce based on coinage and gained their first experience with goods brought in Viking ships from every corner of the known world. It is a measure of the Viking separateness from—and simultaneously their contribution to—Irish life that, although the Scandinavian language was not to permeate Gaelic speech as it did English, some very significant words entered the Irish vocabulary through the Vikings, among them *margad* for "market" and *pingin* for "penny."

For 100 years after the marriage of Olaf the White to a princess of Tara, Irish and Viking life continued its dizzying progression of will-o'-the-wisp alliances and hotheaded animosities. Not until the middle of the 10th Century was any sustained attempt made to put the struggles to rest and forge a stable union that could be called a state. And when that did occur, it originated in an unexpected quarter—not with the Vikings but with the Irish, and in the person of the son of a little-known king of Munster. The son was Brian Boru, who made a life's career of trying to tame Vikings and Irish alike—and he nearly succeeded.

Brian was born about 941 in the Munster countryside, the youngest of 12 brothers who grew up smarting under the sting of raids from the Vikings of Limerick, the major city in the area. And Brian devised deadly counterattacks, springing with his followers from caves and copses to ambush the Vikings on their way to and from the city. In time the Vikings were driven from Limerick, and the provinces of Munster and neighboring Leinster were united under Brian. By 999, after some 25 battles fought over almost four decades, Brian had won sway over all the native Irish kings and had even captured Dublin, making a vassal of Sigtrygg Silkbeard, a one-eyed, half-Norwegian, half-Irish chieftain then ruling Dublin. Soon thereafter Brian was styled Emperor of the Irish.

In that role he brought a blessed end to the fighting. Ruling over a peaceable confederacy of kingdoms, he restored Ireland's devastated churches and founded schools. He built causeways from the sea islands, bridges over the rivers and highways over the land.

But the peace was too frail to last. After barely a decade, one of the Irish kings, Maelmordha of Leinster, reverted to type and plotted to overthrow Brian. In 1012 Maelmordha formed an alliance with Silkbeard, who had never truly accepted Brian's suzerainty. The dampened hostilities flared up, and soon the country was in chaos. The climax came at the Battle of Clontarf—the epic battle of Ireland's war-torn history.

Ireland's social fabric was by now such a patchwork quilt that practically everyone had relatives on the adversaries' side. Sigtrygg had Irish blood from his mother, a princess named Gormflaith, who had been married many times, once to Brian Boru, which made Brian one of Sigtrygg's stepfathers. Sigtrygg, in turn, had married one of Brian's daughters by another Irish wife, which made him a son-in-law of Brian's. To top it off, the rebellious Maelmordha of Leinster was Gormflaith's brother, which made him Brian's brother-in-law and Sigtrygg's uncle.

The political and geographical threads were as tangled as those of the family relationships. An Irish chronicle claimed that opposing Brian was an army "of all the foreigners of the Western world." And indeed, Sigtrygg had sent emissaries to Vikings everywhere, seeking allies and promising rewards of money, land and adventure. To two separate Viking chieftains he offered in marriage his mother (Brian's ex-wife) and for a dowry the city of Dublin. Among those who answered the call were Brodir, ruler of the Isle of Man, a menacing fellow who tucked his long black hair into his belt, and Sigurd the Stout from the Orkneys. Each came with shiploads of warriors, bringing the forces of Sigtrygg and Maelmordha to 20,000. But rallying to Brian's cause were 20,000 warriors representing all the clans of Ireland except those in the rebellious Leinster and a clan or two that remained neutral—plus one foreign Viking, a brother of Brodir's named Ospak, who hated his sibling.

The two great armies came together on Good Friday in April 1014. All day long they fought on a triangular plain at the confluence of the Tolka and the Liffey Rivers, just outside Dublin. When the day was over, 7,000 Leinster rebels and Viking allies were dead, and although the Irish loyalists of Brian Boru lost some 4,000 men themselves, they claimed the victory. But the 73-year-old Brian was not on hand to celebrate. In the late afternoon he had been struck in the head with an ax by Brodir, who according to one account caught the old man as he knelt at prayer in his tent in a nearby wood. Brian's Irish followers took revenge worthy of Vikings by cutting open Brodir's belly, tacking his entrails to a tree and forcing him to march round the trunk until he died.

The Irish ever after celebrated the Battle of Clontarf as the supreme moment of national unity and liberation, the definitive triumph of the great hero Brian Boru over the Leinster separatists and the Vikings. It is true that after Clontarf never again did a major Viking invasion fleet appear off the coast of Ireland. The Vikings apparently accepted the futility of trying to conquer the intractable Irish. But Viking influence was anything but dead in Ireland. The Vikings remained and learned to live in peace with the Irish. A number of them even continued to rule their city kingdoms and, as sagacious traders, brought profit to both themselves and the Irish. The Norwegian half-breed Sigtrygg Silkbeard, for one, survived the disaster of Clontarf and remained on his throne in Dublin all the remaining 20 years of his life.

His heirs, like those of other Viking chieftains, married Irish princesses, until over the years they were assimilated into their adopted land and became as Irish as their mothers. As for their cities, Dublin, Wexford, Waterford and the rest grew and prospered as a legacy of the Viking sojourn in Ireland. Rimming the southerly corner of the island, these cities gave the isolated Irish what they had never had before—a window onto England and the Continent, and the world of trade beyond.

A silver coin minted in Dublin about the year 1000 by Viking King Sigtrygg Silkbeard, whose picture appears on the face, attests to the importance and permanence the Norsemen attached to the cities they founded in Ireland. The Vikings became such a part of Irish life that 150 years after their power had waned in the 11th Century their coins were still accepted throughout the land.

The Viking fathers of the Russian state

As the Norwegians and Danes fought their way to dominance in Western Europe, the Swedes turned their dragon prows to the East, pressing across the Baltic and into a land that promised adventure and trade. Here, among the forests and steppes, lived the less well-organized and ill-armed Slavic tribes, easy prey for sword-swinging Vikings in search of pelts and slaves. And beyond the Slavic settlements, the rivers wound south to the cities of the Byzantine Empire and the terminus of caravan routes to the Orient.

But while some Swedish Vikings, who were also known as Varangians, surged south and east to plunder and trade, many others remained for generations in Russia as rulers. The legend of Viking rule there is related in the *Russian Primary Chronicle*—a fascinating, if often muddled and romanticized, account first inscribed in the 12th Century by Russian Orthodox monks. In the 15th Century, illustrations were added to one version, creating a delightful pictorial history, parts of which, including the Old Church Slavonic text, are reproduced below and on the following pages.

By the Ninth Century, according to the *Chronicle*, the Slavic tribes had developed respect for the strength and ability of Viking traders and raiders they called Rus, a term probably borrowed from the Finnish name for the Swedes. And in 862, says the *Chronicle*, Slavs offered an irresistible invitation to the Rus: "Our land is great and rich, but there is no order in it. Come to rule and reign over us."

A Viking named Rurik answered the plea and set himself up in Novgorod as monarch over a vast area, which, along with regions in the south, became known as the land of the Rus. From Novgorod, continues the *Chronicle*, two of Rurik's lieutenants named Askold and Dir turned south, traveling along rivers and lakes for 600 miles to Kiev.

Kiev had the makings of a major entrepôt between northern Russia and the Byzantine Empire. In 880 Rurik's successor, Oleg, sallied down the Dnieper, deposed Askold and Dir and declared Kiev the "mother of Russian cities." From this new capital, Oleg fortified the Dnieper trade route and extended his suzerainty over Slavs from Novgorod to Kiev.

Vikings put their versatile axes to use building walls around Novgorod, the seat of power of Rurik, the Swedish chieftain who ruled over the primitive Slavic tribes. South of Novgorod, about a dozen towns along the Dnieper grew and prospered from the Vikings' lively river-based trade.

Backed by a boatload of Viking warriors, Askold and Dir approach a Slavic leader in Kiev, seeking information about this settlement on the Dnieper only 300 miles from the Black Sea. The town was a Slavic political and commercial center, and after the Vikings seized it in 862, it grew into one of Europe's greatest cultural and commercial cities.

Seated on a simple, boxlike throne, a Ninth Century Viking ruler accepts pelts as tribute from his Slavic subjects. In the early years of their rule, Vikings levied taxes on the number of plows and hearths a man might have, but by the 10th Century they had devised a system of tax districts under the authority of collection agents.

Vast tribute from the city of golden domes

Though the Viking Oleg expended great effort in consolidating and administering the new Russian state, his lust for adventure remained undiminished. Soon he was pumping the profits from tribute and trade into warships to travel down the Russian rivers toward more distant horizons.

Constantinople, the great gold-domed capital of the Byzantine Empire, was only a fortnight's sail across the Black Sea from the Dnieper. In 907, according to the *Chronicle*, Oleg drew up before Constantinople's harbor, leading a mighty fleet of 2,000 ships carrying 80,000 men.

There, his way was blocked by a great chain. But the clever Oleg, reports the *Chronicle*, brought his ships ashore and had them equipped with wheels. And "when the wind was favorable, they spread sail and bore down upon the city." The overawed Byzantines pleaded for peace and sent Oleg home with a trade treaty and much treasure, including brocade sails for his ships.

But the pinnacle of Viking power in the East was reached by Oleg's grandson Svyatoslav. Beginning in the year 963, he subdued the great Khazar and Bulgar tribes along the Volga and the Danube. In breaking these peoples, Svyatoslav unwittingly opened the land to the Pechenegs, fierce nomadic horsemen from the eastern steppes. And one day he himself was ambushed by the invading Pechenegs, who made a gold-lined cup from his skull and drank to the death of the Russians.

The Byzantine Patriarch Photius dips a cloak reputed to be that of the Virgin Mary into the Black Sea in a desperate attempt to repulse a Viking seaborne attack on Constantinople led by Askold and Dir in 862. According to the Chronicle, the Virgin — protectress of the city — intervened with a severe tempest, "confusing the boats of the godless Rus" and blocking Viking conquest for 50 years.

On proud steeds and in sleek craft, a Viking army closes on Constantinople in a 907 attack engineered by Oleg, ruler of Kiev. Although the mariners were mostly Vikings, the horsemen were quite often mercenaries who were recruited from nomadic steppe tribes. The Vikings also found willing fighters among the Slavs.

With his naval assault at first stymied by a chain across the Bosporus, Oleg unleashes his legions on the outskirts of Constantinople, where an archer executes a pleading prisoner and a soldier sets fire to a church. Oleg's army pillaged and plundered, inflicting, says the Russian Primary Chronicle, "woes upon the Greeks after the usual manner of soldiers."

Surrounded by a sea of grass, Oleg's fleet, fitted out with wheels and propelled by the wind, rolls up to the gates of Constantinople, where terrified Byzantines greet them with trumpets and gestures of peace. According to the Chronicle, the Greeks offered Oleg 12 silver coins for each rowlock in every Russian boat.

Spewing streams of flaming death, the Byzantine army repulses the fleet of Oleg's successor, Igor, who mounted his first attack on Constantinople in 941, possibly in hopes of extracting even more favorable concessions from the Greeks. This Greek fire, which was composed of naphtha, saltpeter and sulfur, and ignited on contact, was squirted out of tubes or hurled in clay pots toward the enemy.

A religion to knit together an empire

By the year 987, the Viking-descended rulers of Russia had managed to beat back the nomadic Pechenegs, and had consolidated their power over the land conquered by Svyatoslav. It was now that Vladimir, son of Svyatoslav, came to the fore. But his contribution was different from that of his volatile Viking predecessors. The men he sent out from the city of Kiev went in search of kingdoms and riches of a far different sort—a religion to unify the burgeoning Russian empire.

The emissaries traveled east, west and south. On their return, they reported a "dreadful stench" in Muslim Bulgaria and said as well that they "beheld no glory" in the churches of Roman Catholic Germany. But the agents could not find words glorious enough to describe the clouds of incense and the ethereal domes of Constantinople's Greek Orthodox churches, where, they said, "we knew not whether we were in heaven or on earth."

Vladimir continued to ponder the matter until 988, when the Byzantine Emperor came forward with a bargain that mingled spiritual salvation with political gain: the Emperor would offer his sister in marriage in exchange for Vladimir's conversion—plus 6,000 troops to squelch an internal rebellion.

Vladimir was baptized that very year, and soon the new religion brought a stream of Greek Orthodox and Bulgarian priests, educators and architects to Russia. Before long, the distinct Viking element would be almost totally absorbed in this new Greco-Slavic culture.

Byzantine clergymen demonstrate religious rituals for the envoys of Vladimir, who is about to bring Russia into the Greek Orthodox Church. Vladimir was to gain a reputation for piety, but before finding solace in his adopted religion, the prince reputedly enjoyed the comfort of seven wives and 800 concubines.

On their return to Kiev, Vladimir's envoys offer a glowing account of the material wealth and spiritual splendor of the Greek Orthodox Church. The men then reminded Vladimir that his grandmother Olga—a true Viking, who once buried some enemies alive—had found divine balm in the Byzantine faith. This crude perspective shows the emissaries seated in each other's laps instead of squarely on the benches.

Crowned by a halo, Vladimir is baptized into the Greek Orthodox faith in a church font in the Greek city of Kherson (top right). Following Vladimir's example, three subjects (bottom right) squeeze into a baptismal font. These fonts were too small for the scale of conversion Vladimir intended. So the zealous new believer ordered his subjects at sword point into the Dnieper for a mass baptism.

С слышавъ володимиръ ре҃ · ащейстина буде ·
то полетищъ же елика въ гробъ а мѣсѣ · иповелѣ кр
стити епⷣа же корсунскый · стопы црчны · ѿ
гласи крти володимира · и иаковъ злы... у кꙋ
пань · на не прозрѣ · и видѣ вкие володимеръ · на
прасное иселение и про сⷬ в ивⷯⷮ ре҃ти рекⷭ ведⷬжⷶ ·

Н еже видѣвши дрⷤхнаⷱ · мнози крⷮиша · крⷮи же ивⷬⷣⷭⷨ
стоевⷯⷭⷭ · иецрⷭⷭ в нестоⷩⷣⷭⷭⷩ · и порⷯⷨⷩ грⷶⷩⷶⷩ мⷭ ⷮⷭⷶ
еⷩⷶ глⷶ · идⷮ на торгъ · повелѣⷮ володимираⷶ в крⷮⷭⷣⷭⷮ
стоⷮⷮ · и доⷱⷣⷩⷶ црⷱⷩⷶ полата рⷶⷶ батⷶ ре · п кре
щⷱⷩⷶ же при ⷭⷶ црⷮⷩ на воⷰⷶ учⷩⷶ ⷭ ·

Chapter 4

Shining the light of commerce on a dark age

Bangles representing the fruits of wide-ranging Viking trade—and plunder—adorn this late-Ninth Century necklace. Two of the more interesting items, interspersed with beads of crystal and semiprecious red carnelian, are a stirrup-shaped Khazar ornament from the lower Volga (upper right) and an oblong book mount of English origin (lower left). Vikings loved every sort of bauble, going "to any length," as one 10th Century Arab observed, "to get hold of colored beads."

he Viking was fond of portraying himself as the ultimate warrior. And quite possibly he was. But there was much more to him than this one-dimensional image. He was, in fact, as much a merchant as marauder and conqueror. His battle sword went hand in hand with the tiny and delicate scales he used to measure the silver that represented commercial gain. And it was in his mercantile endeavors that he made some of his strongest contributions to civilization.

The Scandinavians were traders long before they became Vikings. The initial resource upon which Scandinavian commerce was founded was a marvelous substance that had come as a godsend to the eastern shore of Jutland and the southern Baltic coast. This was amber, the clear, fossilized resin of pine trees that had died millions of years before on land that was, in this case, later covered by the waters of the Baltic. The sea washed it ashore in chunks, and it eventually accumulated in such quantities that several thousand pounds of amber could be extracted from an area encompassing only a few acres. Amber was the diamond of its day, fetching premium prices from European ladies, who loved the golden play of light on the strings of amber beads that they wore on their bosoms. It was rendered even more valuable by the fact that when rubbed it took on a highly magnetic charge, a property that seemed magical. In fact, the English word electricity is derived from the Greek *elektron,* which means "amber."

The Vikings traded in amber almost from the start of their history. As early as the Second Millennium B.C., they were carrying it in crude craft down the coast of the North Sea and into central and southeastern Europe by way of the Elbe and other rivers. And as the Bronze Age faded into the Iron Age, the range and variety of commerce expanded in relation to advances in Norse shipbuilding sciences. The Viking longship and its commercial cousins, the variously sized knarrs, all of them highly maneuverable, enabled the Viking to probe trade routes never before open to merchant traffic.

Indeed, it required no conflict of identity for the Viking to lay aside his sword and pick up his scales. To realize a profit from his plunder, the Norse raider sold it in the marketplace. It was said of one of the characters in a saga, a merchant named Thorolf Kveldulfsson, that he divided his time between Viking raids and trading voyages—and the two were often indistinguishable: a Viking merchant bound for the marketplace did not hesitate to turn pirate if he spotted weaker commercial shipping along the way.

This raid-and-trade duality was manifest in many ways and on many occasions. When Viking freebooters established a settlement on the island of Noirmoutier near the estuary of the River Loire in 842, they had more in mind than a base for raids into France. Noirmoutier was situated in an area of fine vineyards and extensive marshes whose waters, when drained and channeled into separate, shallow retaining basins, could be allowed to evaporate, leaving layers of salt. Since Roman times, Noirmoutier had been a center for trade in wines and salt—and the Vikings simply took over the franchise.

Three years later, Danes directed by a king named Horik staged one of the most spectacular of all Viking invasions. Horik was an exceedingly ruthless leader, as witness the fact that he survived as ruler of a notably unruly people for 27 years. He was also of eminently pragmatic mind, and he realized that both power and wealth could be better attained by massed forces than by the individual, glory-seeking forays that the Vikings so loved.

In 845, therefore, Horik put together a fleet numbered by contemporary count at some 600 vessels—which, even allowing for generous exaggeration, must surely have been an awesome armada. The target was Hamburg, key to the Elbe, and Horik's Danes burst through its massive quadrangular wall in a frenzy of destruction; when they were done, according to accounts of the time, no single stone in the town remained standing upon another. Yet they left untouched the most vulnerable target of all: the wooden houses and shops of the merchants' quarters along the river, outside the wall and completely undefended. The omission could only have been deliberate, probably by Horik's direct order. Whether any Vikings actually made use of the market area is unknown; if they did, it was only briefly. For Horik's main force soon ventured up the Elbe into the interior, where it was soundly defeated and driven from the land by an army of Saxons.

On such occasions the Viking raider was clearly an instrument of calculated commercial policy—and as such, he was a vital force, a light leading toward the end of the Dark Ages that had befallen the world with the collapse of the Roman Empire and with the Eighth Century Muslim assault on the Mediterranean world. Communications were disrupted, commerce withered, and the kingdoms of Western Europe entered a long and gloomy time of despond. Europe, which had boasted great provinces with opulent courts and thriving cities, became for the most part a collection of backward, subsistence-level communities, each ruled by a petty feudal lord whose vision seldom extended further than his neighbor's barn.

To this stagnant society the Northmen in their swift ships brought mobility, quickening the sluggish pace of life and reopening the windows of trade. In the Old World the Vikings were not discoverers in the true sense of the word—that would come with their voyages to the New World. Instead, the Viking achievement in Europe was to take a patchwork of separate and disparate waterways, many of them long unused or even forgotten, and organize them into a network within which men and goods might move from the Middle East to the British Isles.

Knotting the strands of this commercial network and making a whole of the parts were the Norse trading towns, shrewdly situated so as to provide both accessibility to merchants and tactical protection against marauders, yet also located, with a sweeping strategic sense, at vital commercial crossroads.

In foreign lands, the Vikings often set up fortified strongholds and later converted them to international market towns, as was the case with Dublin, Limerick, Cork, Waterford and Wexford in Ireland. Sometimes established towns—York in England and Rouen in Normandy—were turned by the Northmen to their own mercantile use. In Russia, the settlements of Kiev, Rostov and Novgorod came into being as Viking

trading outposts. Within Scandinavia itself, where Viking preyed upon Viking, special care was taken to locate the towns where they were safe from easy attack. Thus Norway's Kaupang lay on the shores of a bay where islands, shoals and narrow channels made the approaches slow and hazardous for marauding strangers and effectively prevented surprise assault. Denmark's Hedeby, oldest and largest of the towns, was even more favorably situated at the southern base of the Jutland peninsula, separated from the open Baltic by 25 miles of the Schlei inlet and guarded by elaborate man-made defenses (pages 98-100). But of them all, the town with the most secure natural position, and the most exciting trade, was Sweden's Birka, located deep in the heart of the land, along waterways that gave access to both the treasures of the North and those of Russia and the East.

The town of Birka was probably founded around the year 800 by Vikings from Sweden, who used it both as a marketplace for local commerce and as a collection point for the rich northern fur trade that was then springing up. But such was Birka's location and such was the rapid rise of Viking trade that within a period of 25 years the town became a major enterprise whose commercial arteries spread for hundreds of miles to all points of the compass.

Birka was located on a great lake called Mälar, which offered seven major entrances and exits. The Vikings were able to travel east into the Gulf of Finland and on to the Volga River, or east and then north to rivers that would take them to the White Sea, or south to prosperous Gotland and Hedeby, and beyond to England and Frisia, or west by at least two river-and-lake routes into Middle Sweden, or north by sea or by a series of lakes, rivers and glacial moraines by boat, horse and foot to fur-rich hunting grounds.

Yet one of the great values of Birka was that all these waterways leading out to the world were narrow and easily defended against invaders seeking to enter. No force of any size could come upon Birka without warning. Any vessel approaching by the eastern entrance from the Baltic, for example, would first have to thread its way through a bewildering 30-mile maze of islands, skerries and rocky shoals east of where Stockholm lies today. The vessel would then traverse a cramped bottleneck strait, which finally opened onto a vast lake, itself some 80 miles long and averaging about 13 miles in its breadth. The ship would have to skim across the shallow waters, twisting and turning among the lake's 1,200 islands, for another 18 miles before arriving at the island of Björkö. There, at last, would be Birka.

Guarding the approach to the town was an outcropping of rock 100 feet high, falling sheer into the lake on its western side and protected on the north, the east and the south by a rampart of earth and stone, six feet high and 20 to 40 feet across. The enclosure served as refuge for the town's inhabitants during time of attack, and atop the rock stood a fort from which watchmen could see approaching enemy ships for many miles in all directions.

The town itself, spread over 32 acres, was located a quarter mile to the north on a promontory, and its bustle began at the water's edge—or even

Portable bronze scales, such as these that folded neatly into a bronze container no larger than a man's palm, were indispensable to Viking merchants, who traded their wares for precisely measured amounts of silver and gold. Traders exchanged coins by the weight of precious metal, not denomination, and kept a supply of chopped-up coins (below) on hand to put the scales into perfect balance.

Hedeby: a thriving metropolis in the pagan North

A much-traveled Moorish merchant named Ibraham ibn Ahmed Al-Tartushi visited the Danish trading city of Hedeby in the 10th Century while on a trip into the wild Viking North. He described it as an appalling place, noisy and filthy, where the barbaric inhabitants hung animal sacrifices on poles in front of their houses, and subsisted chiefly on fish, "for there was so much of it."

Hedeby may not have compared with the Moorish splendor of the sophisticated merchant's native Cordoba. But it was the premier metropolis of the Viking age in Scandinavia and, despite Al-Tartushi's scorn, rich in the goods of Viking trade: jewelry, hides, fabrics, glass and slaves.

Like Sweden's Birka and other important market centers, Hedeby owed its existence to two factors: proximity to primary trade routes and natural defenses. Hedeby was located on the eastern shore of the narrow Jutland peninsula, with access to sea routes west across Europe and east into the Baltic. Merchants from the west unloaded their cargoes at a tiny port opposite Hedeby and trundled their goods in oxcarts 10 miles across the peninsula to the town, protected from robbers by a system of earthworks (top center).

The town itself was blessed by its location on a protected

bay, Haddeby Noor, and by a beach where small craft could be landed for loading, unloading or repair. Heavier ships tied up to a curved, strongly built wooden breakwater.

The breakwater was an extension of a rugged semicircular rampart that protected Hedeby from assault by the ever-present outlaw gangs, or by the forces of rival kings. The walls were 30 feet high, made of timber, and were pierced by three gateways or tunnels (far left, far right and top center), each six feet wide and topped by a wooden watchtower. A deep moat ran along the outside of the walls.

Between the rampart and the town was open space, where itinerant merchants and peddlers pitched their tents while doing business with Hedeby's permanent tradesmen. Water for the town came from wells and from a stream through the center of town whose banks were walled with wood to prevent erosion.

Hedeby was founded around 800 when three small villages united. It grew to 60 acres and flourished for 250 years despite all perils, its narrow streets (overleaf) alive with all the vigor of the Viking age. At last, in the year 1050, King Harald Hardradi of Norway, at war with the Danes, burned it to the ground. It was never completely rebuilt.

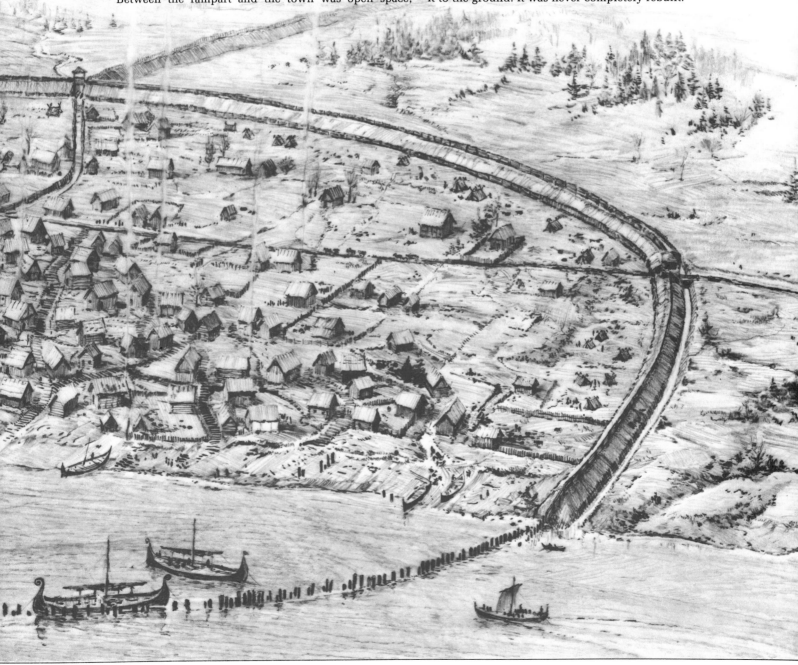

Swarming visitors after the spring thaw

People and animals surge through a narrow street in Hedeby, its walkway of boards covering the mud of the spring thaw. During this season the town's population of 1,000 began to explode as perhaps twice that number of traders, like the Arab slaver in the foreground (whose gloomy chattels include a young girl and a monk) came by sea and land to barter with Hedeby's merchants and artisans.

One such craftsman at right works the horns of stags and reindeer into combs and knife handles while a nearby blacksmith tends his fire. Householders behind the artisans repair winter damage on their 10-foot-square wattle-and-daub dwellings. In the background a two-oared boat off-loads merchandise on the bank of the stream that flows through town. Pigs and goats are being taken to market—for the people, despite Al-Tartushi's snobbish remarks, ate pork and lamb as well as fish.

before, as men either waded or put out in small boats to load and unload merchant ships tied to oak pilings driven into a shallow bar lying off the town. Behind the bar, the water deepened into the main harbor, its jetties crowded with ships. There were two other harbors on the promontory, one suitable for use by cargo vessels, and the other a shallow artificial basin, possibly used as a sort of floating open-air mart for local merchandise brought by light boats.

Crowding down to Birka's beaches, small wattle-and-daub houses and larger buildings of timber caulked with clay and moss sheltered not only permanent residents but transients, who numbered perhaps 1,000 at the height of the trading season. Buyers and sellers alike, haggling in as many as a dozen tongues, thronged the timber boardwalks and jostled each other in the dirt streets. Swedes and Danes and Norwegians, bumpkins from the surrounding countryside and Viking warriors fresh from gory expeditions, hunters from the frozen north and ironmongers from the lake regions, Gotland Islanders and Åland Islanders, sleek Greeks and swarthy Arabs of the East and Spain, Dnieper Slavs and Rhineland Germans, Irish and English, Franks and Frisians—all were there, many of them deadly enemies in any other setting, but here united in the common coin of trade.

Chaotic though the scene may have seemed, there was a form of order, imposed by local law. Under ordinary Swedish law, there was a sliding scale of penalties for various crimes. A man convicted of killing someone from his own province might be forced to compensate the victim's kin with a large amount of blood money. But if a man killed someone from another province, the required payment in blood money was much less. As for foreigners, they could be murdered without penalty. Clearly, this inequity could not be permitted to continue if Birka was to attract merchants from foreign lands, and the so-called Law of Birka was adopted to guarantee safe conduct and equal protection to all. Precisely how much blood money was demanded for murder is not known, but it was the same for strangers as for residents; assault and battery cost 10 marks across the board, while theft was punishable by a fine of three marks. The law was enforced by the local Swedish ruler and his minions, in return for which he was awarded the right to purchase newly imported goods three days ahead of anyone else—in effect, giving him control over higher quality merchandise.

Under the protective canopy of the Law of Birka, local traders and overseas merchants met on equal footing, and the fruit of Viking plunder mixed higgledy-piggledy with honest wares—and no questions asked. There was little trade in heavy bulk cargoes, particularly over long distances. To be sure, Birka did export some of Sweden's good iron ore. But Viking vessels were not really built to carry such weight, and neither at that time were the tubby roundships, or cogs, used by the Saxons, Frisians and Franks of Western Europe. Instead, the iron ore was generally refined on the spot immediately after it was extracted from the mines, which were north of Birka; the smelted iron was then beaten into bars and transported by pack animal to the smithies of Birka, where it was fashioned into tools and weapons, which could either be used locally or handily exported.

To Birka by small boat came farmers with barley, fish, meat and other foodstuffs, which were used both to sustain the Birka community and to supply outgoing merchant ships. These commodities were usually bartered, often for items that had been brought by the same ships—German quernstones for grinding grain, household bowls made from easily carved Norwegian soapstone, and the decorative brooches that were a popular substitute for buttons.

But the island trading town would never have been established as a mere neighborhood exchange: Birka owed its existence to the adventurous and acquisitive instincts that caused Vikings to look longingly toward foreign shores and wealthy lands, and to the seafaring skills that took them there. The Northmen exported a variety of goods that could be handily carried and turned to a profit—horsehides and goatskins, sword hilts, feathers, walrus ivory for holy objects, walnuts and hazel nuts and even acorns.

One of the most prized items was reindeer antler horn. The reindeer migrated in huge herds from woodlands where they fed upon lichens in wintertime to valleys where they browsed on fresh green growth in spring and summer to coastal areas where, in autumn, they devoured marine algae cast up on the beaches. During these migrations, the herds

The aggressive commercial pursuits of the Norsemen are memorialized in these lively woodcuts from a 16th Century Nordic history by Swedish cleric Olaus Magnus. In the top panels, Norsemen hunt the seemingly inexhaustible numbers of fur-bearing animals of the northern forests and land mammoth fish. In the lower left panel, trade goods lie in neat bales on shore, and merchants portage their craft to bypass the rapids of a Russian river as they make their way to a rich Eastern market. At lower right, hunters and traders haggle enthusiastically.

could be harried into cul-de-sacs or tricked into corrals by tame reindeer decoys. To the Laplander, who followed behind the herds and domesticated some of the animals, the reindeer supplied milk and meat, and skin for clothing. The animal was at once a beast of burden and a measurement of wealth. In the Norse mercantile world, reindeer horn was a valuable commodity to be carved into ornate combs or sword mounts and sold at high prices.

But of all the natural resources upon which the Viking traders drew for their exports, the greatest bounty came from furs. For part of its prosperity, the town of Birka could be grateful for its convenient location, which provided access to the pine and birch forests of the North, where warm-coated animals scurried and burrowed and climbed and swam in numberless millions.

The nobility, the higher clergy and the rich merchant class of Europe were never able to get enough of the Norse pelts with which they could flaunt their wealth and grandeur, and Adam of Bremen spoke with the thunderous voice of official Christian morality when he denounced "strange furs, the odor of which has inoculated our world with the deadly poison of pride. To our shame, we hanker after a martenskin robe as much as for supreme happiness."

He was wasting his words. And to satisfy the unsated and insatiable appetite for furs, Birka—unlike such other market towns as Kaupang, Hon and Truso—remained open year round. Indeed winter, when the pelts came into their prime, was a peak season. Then the northern hunters and trappers, using long skis and flat skates made of the haunch bones of cows, on which they propelled themselves by leaning on pointed sticks, could skim down snow-packed hills and along frozen waterways; with them went bale-piled sledges drawn by horses whose hooves were fitted with ice crampons.

The great piles of precious furs made for a sight best described by a traveler: "Beaver and sable past counting, such great bales of ermine that it was impossible to tell how many furs they contained; shiny Siberian squirrel; ruby-colored fox; lynxskins like a springtime meadow sprinkled with hundreds of thousands of violets that could light up a bedroom like the first rays of daylight penetrating the shadows of the night."

In exchange for these treasured natural resources, the Northmen sought equally luxurious goods of a sort to bring pleasure to their days and light to the darkness of their long winter. Aside from such implements as they did not produce themselves—the quernstones, for instance—they had little interest in importing everyday wares for, as Adam of Bremen reported, "they manage to live off their livestock, using the milk for food and the skin and wool for clothing." Instead, among the items offered on any given day in Birka and the other trading towns there could be found brocades from the Byzantine Empire; soft woolen fabrics dyed blue with woad from Frisia; meticulous Anglo-Saxon embroideries; shimmering patterned silk from China (the Vikings introduced the material to England, and the word silk is probably derived from the Old Norse *silki*); ornately worked Arab harnesses and handsomely crafted leather belts studded with metal plaques from Persia; big, two-handled ceramic jars filled with flowery white wines from Germany's

Rhineland; tinted Frankish glass and little glass gaming pieces from the Near East and flattened glass oblongs from Egypt, which could be used to press the pleats of fine linen skirts.

Among all things, the Viking most thirsted for precious metals. Gold he loved when he was able to get it; he had threads of it sewn into his clothing and he sometimes used it for spectacular displays, as when King Olaf Tryggvason of Norway covered the prow and stern of his warship, the *Long Serpent*, with gold leaf. Gold, however, was in short supply, and it was therefore in silver that the Viking found full release for his passion. Silver was relatively plentiful, and with it he could accumulate land or gather followers or amass prestige; it gleamed and glinted when he wore it on his person; and it was high in value, small in bulk and easy to transport.

The Viking coveted silver in all its forms, whether it was a crucifix wrested from an Irish altar or a cup bought from a Syrian merchant or a brooch fashioned by a silversmith of the Khazars, who controlled the banks of the lower Volga. Wherever he was, he collected silver coins. To him, they were without face value. Instead, their worth, as with all other silver, was measured by weight; a basic unit amounted to a bit more than four grams. To make change, he often chopped coins into halves or quarters which, along with fragments of silver ornaments and shavings from rings, were called hacksilver. When a man accumulated enough hacksilver, he often had it melted into bars of standard weight, which were a valid medium of exchange—although there were swindlers who were not above disguising iron bars with a thin coating of silver, to fool unwary customers.

In times of danger, when the Viking feared for the safety of his property, he would place his silver in a bundle and bury it. Sometimes he was killed before he could return to reclaim it, and hundreds of such hoards have been found in Viking lands.

No matter how long the journey or how hazardous the way, the Vikings would seek after silver—and with the late-Eighth or early-Ninth Century discovery of rich deposits in the Kufic region of Mesopotamia, the trail pointed east. That, for the Swedes, was a blessing. To get to the East from their trading center at Birka, the Swedish Vikings had only to sail past the island villages that would one day become the city of Stockholm and set a straight course across the Baltic to the Gulf of Finland. From there, the twisting Neva River carried the ships 43 miles past reefs and through rapids to Lake Ladoga, Europe's largest lake, in the north of Russia some 40 miles east of modern Leningrad. Some of the traders settled there, setting up shop and living among Finnish speaking Slavs. The Slavs called the traders *Ruotsi*, the Finnish word for Swedes; that was eventually corrupted into Rus and became the generic term for the Swedish traders and warriors who gave their name to Russia when they pushed on southward to conquer and rule the vast lands of the Slavs *(pages 88-93)*.

There were some 70 streams feeding Lake Ladoga, but by far the most important to the Rus was the Volkhov River, which led to Lake Ilmen in the south and to the fortified trading town of Novgorod. From there, the Rus rowed—the waterway was too narrow and too swift for them to

In their lust for wealth, the Viking traders accumulated treasures from all over the world. From the Rhineland came this dark-gray ceramic wine jug and funnel-shaped drinking glass. The bronze brazier with tongs was made by Arabian artisans. And though there is no record that the Vikings ever reached the Orient, they traded for quantities of the shimmering silks seen in the contemporary Chinese painting at right.

maneuver through it by sail—farther south, up the River Lovat until they arrived at a point where, by dragging their vessels on log rollers a short distance overland, they were able to reach the source of either of two great rivers. The first was the Dnieper River, winding 1,400 miles to the Black Sea, along whose coast the travelers made their way to Byzantium; the second was the Volga River, flowing some 2,400 miles to the Caspian Sea, where the Viking merchant-mariners joined, of all things, Muslim camel caravans to Baghdad.

The journeys, as described by the Byzantine Emperor Constantine Porphyrogenitus in about 950, were desperately difficult, especially along the Dnieper below Kiev, where the river turns southward through granite gorges and plunges onward in a series of savage cataracts. "In the middle of it," wrote Constantine, "there are sheer high rocks, which look like islands; when the water reaches them and dashes against them it causes a loud and terrifying tumult as it crashes down. Therefore the Rus do not dare sail between them, but lay their boats alongside the bank before this point and make the people go up on shore, though they leave the cargo on board. Then they walk into the water naked, testing the bottom with their feet so as not to stumble over stones; at the same time they thrust the boat forward with poles, many of them at the bows, many amidships, and others at the stern. With all these precautions they wade through the edge of these first rapids, close along the bank; as soon as they have passed them, they take the rest of the crew back on board, and go on their way by boat."

Living and working in their Russian wilderness, the Rus were nothing if not single-minded in their purpose. "Their only business," wrote an Arab geographer and traveler named Ibn Rustah, "is to trade in sable and squirrelskins and other kinds of skin, selling them to those who will buy from them. In payment, they take coins, which they keep in their belts." Another Arab, the diplomat-merchant Ibn Fadlan, was more detailed in his description of the Rus traders: "When their ships arrive at their anchorage, each man goes ashore taking with him bread, meat, leeks, milk and beer, and goes to a tall upright wooden post with a face that looks like a man's. So he goes up to the big figure, flings himself on the ground, and says: 'O my Lord, I have come from far off with so many sableskins' (here he counts up all the wares he has brought), 'and now I come to you with this offering.' (Thereupon he lays what he has brought in front of the wooden post.) 'I pray that you should send me a merchant who has many dinars and dirhems, who will buy from me as I wish, and will not contradict what I say.' "

For more than 150 years, Sweden (and Birka) thrived in the East, becoming the major Scandinavian repository—and, through Danish Hedeby, the dispersal point to the West—for Kufic silver. But during the latter part of the 10th Century, the Kufic mines were exhausted; the Rus chieftains, through the inexorable process of assimilation, became as much Slav as Swede, and their internecine wars disrupted the Eastern trade routes; and around 980, as its silver flow dried to a trickle, Birka was abandoned. By then, the major Scandinavian trade effort had turned back to the West—which Norway, facing toward the North Sea, had always considered its domain.

Odin's gift of writing and sorcery

For all their spectacular achievements as warriors, mariners and merchants, the Vikings left remarkably few written records. But when they did inscribe their words—on gravestones, road markers, weapons or amulets—the Norsemen wrote exclusively in runes, the ancient, magical letters of the gods.

According to Viking legend, the runic (from the Old Norse rūn, meaning "mystery") alphabet was the gift of Odin, the god of warriors, poetry and sorcery. Driven by his passion for knowledge, Odin, though wounded, hung from the wind-swept branches of a tree for nine days and nights to discover the secret of runic writing. The legend does not say how Odin was wounded, or on whom he was spying, only that with a command of runes Odin grew more powerful, and eventually passed his knowledge along to mortals.

The actual origin of the runic alphabet is equally vague. Runes have been variously ascribed to the Greeks, Etruscans, Romans, even the Goths. But the discovery of runelike writing in northern Italy's Dolomite region indicates that the writing probably originated with an unknown Alpine people sometime in the First Century B.C. It was taken up by wandering Germanic tribes early in the Christian Era, adapted to the Teutonic language and carried north to Scandinavia around the Third Century.

By the Ninth Century the Viking runic alphabet was composed of the 16 letters shown below. Each served both as a means of spelling and as the symbol of an object or concept. Used with other letters, "F,"

for example, would spell a word; standing alone it meant cattle. Reading from left to right, the other 15 runes stood for manly strength, giant, god, journey, torch, hail, need, ice, year, bow of yew wood, sun, the god Tīw of war, birch twig, man and water.

As the only literation of Old Norse, runes were inscribed on wood, metal and stone throughout Viking realms to record places and events deemed important in daily life. "Ragnalv had this bridge made in memory of her good son," reads the somewhat ambiguous legend on an 11th Century Swedish stone. "May God help his spirit and soul better than he deserved."

And since runes were the gifts of Odin the Sorcerer, they were presumed to possess a deep and powerful magic. Runes carved in small sticks were used for blessings, spells, curses and divination.

The power runes exerted was great indeed, according to the saga of the Viking hero and poet Egil Skallagrimsson. One day Egil came upon a young girl who lay seriously ill. When he learned that she had an ardent but unsuccessful suitor, Egil immediately suspected witchcraft, and soon uncovered a whalebone inscribed with 10 runes hidden in her bed. Destroying these runes and writing new ones, Egil quickly cured the girl. As it turned out, no malice had been intended by the suitor. He was a novice in the art of runes and had merely made an error in his writing. Thus, according to the saga, came Egil to issue this poetic warning: "Let no man carve runes to cast a spell,/Save first he learns to read them well."

ᚠ	ᚢ	ᚦ	ᚬ	ᚱ	ᚴ	ᚼ	ᚾ	ᛁ	ᛅ	ᛦ	ᛋ	ᛏ	ᛒ	ᛘ	ᛚ
f	u	th	o	r	k	h	n	i	a	R	s	t	b	m	l

ᛋ	ᛁ	ᚴ	ᛚ	ᛏ
s	i	k	l	t

Reading from the serpent's head to its tail, this Swedish runestone memorializes a Baltic merchant with the words: "He often sailed to Semgallen in a dear-prized knarr round Domesnas"—Domesnas being the headlands of the Gulf of Riga, and Semgallen a thriving Viking colony in what is now Latvia. The runes highlighted in the lower right-hand corner spell out phonetically the Old Norse "siklt," which is related to the verb "seglode" in Old English, which eventually became "sailed" in Modern English.

A trade route gave Norway its name: the great North Way ran more than 1,500 miles from the White Sea in the north to Kaupang, the country's main merchant town, on Oslofjord in the south. The journey was slow—it required some six weeks, even when aided by fair winds—but to a Viking navigator who knew the waters it was relatively free of natural hazard. The Norse mariners passed between thousands of small islands, so thickly clustered as to form a breakwater against heavy seas; always they kept the jagged coast of the Norwegian mainland in sight on the port side. The precipitous coastal cliffs were broken by scores of deepwater fjords, and these offered shelter from storm and hiding from pirates—of whom there were plenty.

The Vikings never scrupled to prey on one another, and the Norwegians, perhaps because their native land had been less generously endowed with natural resources than the rest of Scandinavia, were especially rapacious, both in their home waters and in distant lands. Wrote Adam of Bremen: "Forced by the poverty of their homeland they venture far into the world to bring back from their raids the goods that other countries so plentifully produce."

At Kaupang—the name is related to the English name Chipping, which means market town—the trader would put into a small bay that forms a fine natural harbor on the west side of the great Oslofjord. Much less elaborate in its installations than either the towns of Hedeby or Birka, Kaupang was evidently used only as a summer marketplace, where merchants would peddle their wares from turf-walled, roofless booths, which were sometimes tented over with the woolen sailcloth from the Vikings' ships.

Yet for all its lack of show, Kaupang was an important center for one of the most popular of Scandinavian products: steatite, or soapstone, which could be fashioned into such utilitarian trade items as loom weights, lamps, bowls and cooking ware. The Kaupang area was blessed with natural outcroppings of this soapstone, so soft and workable that the utensils could be shaped from the living rock in much the same way that wood is carved. But the greatest business of Kaupang was in receiving the wealth of the North, and there sending it east to Birka in Sweden, south to Hedeby in Denmark and southwest to the trading towns of England and Ireland.

From the late-Ninth Century travels of a Viking named Ottar, the activities of the Norwegian trader may be extrapolated. Like so many of his countrymen, Ottar was a man of several parts: farmer (20 head of cattle, 20 sheep and 20 pigs), reindeer breeder (his herd of 600 included six valuable tame decoys), hunter, mariner and, of course, merchant. During his journeys from his holdings in Halogaland, one of Norway's northernmost provinces, Ottar somehow encountered the English King Alfred the Great of Wessex. The meeting probably occurred a little after 870, when Alfred had a need for ivory and sealhides; cut into strips, these made excellent ship ropes. Though the Anglo-Saxon King had spent much of his life warring against Vikings who sought to seize his land, he nevertheless maintained friendly relations with those who wished only to conduct peaceable commerce. Alfred must have been powerfully impressed by Ottar's tales of his life and adventures, for he had one of his

Dazzling baubles to please a warrior's wife

Viking women, though living in turbulent times and a harsh environment, loved luxuries such as jewelry just as much as the women of any other age or clime. By the year 900 Scandinavian metalsmiths had learned to please them with striking ornaments made of the precious metals that raiding and trading husbands were bringing back from every corner of the known world.

The Viking women naturally doted on necklaces like the one below. No less did they treasure brooches (*right, top and bottom*) as well as those peculiarly Viking arm rings (*far right, top and bottom*) that men also wore and sometimes used as cash for trading purposes.

The hallmark of all this jewelry was its dazzling intricacy of design, as if the craftsmen felt compelled to fill every square millimeter with loops and whorls and ring-chain patterns. Most of the designs include animal figures. Some ornaments have dragon heads, like those on the prows of warships; some pay homage to the sea with fish motifs.

But many show an elongated animal, part reptile, part weasel, part cat, that art historians call the "gripping beast" since, as several of them writhe and coil through a design, they grip one another with their paws. Even when artfully crafted of precious metals, these curious beasts symbolized the ferocity and power of early Norse civilization.

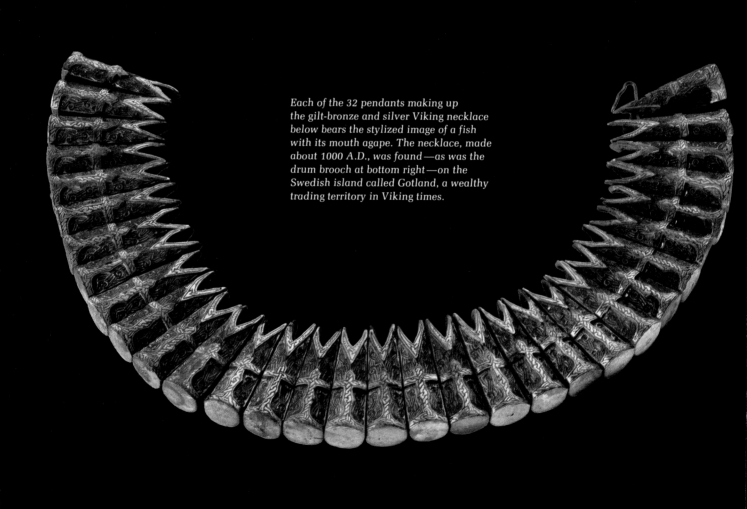

Each of the 32 pendants making up the gilt-bronze and silver Viking necklace below bears the stylized image of a fish with its mouth agape. The necklace, made about 1000 A.D., was found—as was the drum brooch at bottom right—on the Swedish island called Gotland, a wealthy trading territory in Viking times.

A magnificent gold brooch made in Jutland in the early 10th Century fairly writhes with snakelike animals and tendrils. Brooches were not only ornaments but also necessities for well-to-do Viking women, since they were used to fasten the shoulder straps of woolen gowns. Men also wore brooches but of a plainer design.

A coiled silver snake forms the design for this 11th Century arm bracelet that was presumably for a child, since it is only three inches in diameter. The serpent's head is worked in relief and the back is etched to simulate the reptile's skin.

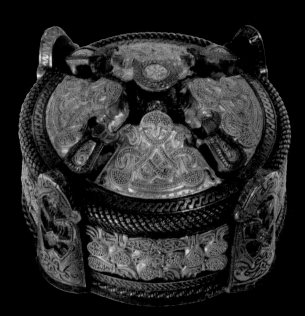

The rich decoration of this drum brooch, which probably belonged to a well-off Gotland woman, appears to be solid gold and silver. But the complex design of the precious metals is in fact only a thin veneer coating a base of bronze.

Two dragon heads snarl at each other from the open ends of this silver arm bracelet. Entwined dragons and a delicate, twisted chain form the rest of the bracelet, which was probably made for a wealthy Gotland woman during the 11th Century.

court scribes write down the stories, and later published them as part of a history of the world.

One of the main sources of Ottar's income was the tribute—in the form of valuable trade goods—exacted from Lapp tribesmen who came from farther north and east to hunt in his Halogaland territory: "Each pays according to his rank," advised Alfred. "The highest in rank must pay fifteen martens' skins, and five of reindeer, and one bearskin, and ten measures of feathers, a kirtle of bearskin or otterskin, and two ship's cables; each must be sixty ells long, the one to be made of whale's hide, the other of seal's."

The furs were, of course, a major item on any Viking lading list. The feathers were in all likelihood the down of the eider, a large black-and-white duck that flocked by the millions throughout the northern lands. The Norsemen as well as the Lapps took the fullest advantage of the bird's quaint nesting habits. The gatherers of down cunningly arranged four stones in such a way as to appear—at least to a female eider—as a convenient nesting place. Once she had decided to move in, the duck would set about busily using her bill to pluck down from her own breast to serve as a soft lining for her new home. When her eggs were laid, she would cover them with another layer of down—at which point the human hunters would steal the eggs, which were eaten as a delicacy, and collect the down.

But the eider was a dauntless duck. Back the female would come to pluck more down and lay more eggs; and back the hunters would come for another harvest. The unequal contest continued until, as the nesting season neared its end, the duck laid her last batch. These the hunters allowed to hatch, refraining from filching the down until the young had left the nest—thereby maintaining the priceless eider population. Soft, light and elastic, the down fetched premium prices for pillows and quilts throughout Europe.

As for ship's cables, which were made from the tough yet supple skin of whales, seals and other sea mammals, they were without a doubt the strongest and most durable rigging in the world. Both the Vikings and the Laplanders fashioned them by cutting a single spiral strip out of the animal's hide from the shoulder to the tail—and it was reported that the resulting cables or ropes were so strong that they could not be pulled apart in a tug of war between 60 men.

How successful Ottar and the other Viking hunters were as whalers is a matter of conjecture. Alfred's account of Ottar's activities describes whales that were "fifty ells long. He said that in company with five other crews he killed sixty of these in two days."

Since 50 ells would have been 187 feet and no known whale has ever approached that length, it may be assumed that Ottar was telling a Viking fish story. His monsters were probably right whales, which grow as long as 65 feet. The Vikings hunted them from small boats. They would hector the huge, air-breathing mammals into shallow coves; there, floundering and unable to maneuver, the whales were harpooned. Even if Ottar killed only 1/10 the number that he claimed, his reward would still have been immense.

The Vikings knew how to boil the oil from whale blubber, and a single

Two of the greatest prizes the arctic seas had to offer, a narwhal and a walrus, display their heavy ivory tusks in this illustration from a 17th Century guide to Iceland's fauna. The Vikings sold the walrus tusks to ecclesiastics for crucifixes and to warriors for sword grips, among other things. But the greatest profit was in the narwhal's long whorled tusk, which could be sold as the horn of a unicorn.

right whale would yield 275 barrels of the precious fluid; the oil was used for illumination, all manner of lubrication and for treating leather. There would also be 3,000 pounds of whalebone, the flexible bonelike structure in the whale's mouth through which the animal strained its plankton food; this was immensely valuable as belt buckles, knife handles and spades. Finally, the right whale would offer ton upon ton of rich, dark-red, beeflike meat.

There was still another whale, actually a member of the porpoise family, which Ottar may not have mentioned to Alfred—with good reason, since part of the beast's anatomy was used in a common Viking deception. This was the narwhal. The beast itself attained a length of only about 16 feet, but it grew from its upper jaw a straight, spirally grooved tusk that extended as far as eight feet, with a nine-inch girth at the base. Despite this awesome growth—probably a secondary sexual characteristic similar to a rooster's comb—the narwhal was a timid animal, not difficult to hunt down and kill. The Vikings would fob the grotesque tusk off upon gullible buyers as the horn of a unicorn, a fabled horselike creature that held human imagination in thrall for centuries (pages 112-113).

There was another animal the Vikings pursued that boasted tusks of solid, gleaming ivory, much like those of an elephant. These were truly valuable. The animal was the walrus, which lived in great herds in the White Sea east around the tip of Norway. A trip that far to the north was a dangerous journey even in the summer; aside from everything else, hunting the walrus was risky. The huge, benign-looking beasts were placid enough when they were left undisturbed, but when threatened they became fiercely aggressive. The Vikings, like the Eskimo hunters of the far north, attempted to drive the creatures into the shallow water, where their aquatic ability was diminished, or catch them on the ice, where their vast bulk rendered their escape difficult. But many a hunter received injury or was killed by the flailing flippers, the huge tail and the sharp-pointed tusks 18-inches long.

There was one other commodity the Vikings dealt in, and it brought them the greatest profit of all—more than amber or silver, or pelts, whether whale or walrus. It was neither manufactured by man nor dug from the earth nor fished from the sea nor slain on land. That commodity was human beings. For, during the days of their dominance, the Vikings were slavers to the world.

The Vikings certainly did not invent the insidious institution of slavery—it had existed in prehistory—but they exploited it on a scale unknown to any north European people before them. The survivors of those vanquished in battle automatically became subject to servitude. Slavs in the East and, though they had a dangerous tendency to rise against their masters, the Irish and the English in the West were especially valued for their strength. Nor were Scandinavians by any means safe from other Scandinavians. Women found to be unchaste, undischarged debtors, and men who would otherwise have been condemned to die by the ax for crimes real or imagined, were all candidates for slavery. To wind up on the losing side in one of the Vikings' innumerable blood feuds was a sure way to the marketplace. Indeed, feud or no feud, all that was really necessary was to be taken unawares.

"As soon as one has caught his neighbor," wrote the church chronicler Adam of Bremen about the Vikings, "he sells him ruthlessly as a slave, to either friend or stranger."

Under Norse masters, the slave by law and by custom was treated as little more than a farm animal, fit mostly to spread dung in the fields, dig peat, herd goats and tend pigs. Under the 10th Century Norwegian Frostathing Law every landed family was required to send a certain number of men to fight for the king when called, and the law suggested how many slaves might be necessary to keep the farm running in their absence. A medium-sized farm, one of perhaps a dozen cows and two horses, advised the law, might require three slaves, while the estate of a lord would need 30 or more to operate efficiently. In England, if one man killed another man's slave he was required to pay the owner the equivalent value in cows: eight. Under such a system of values, it was inevitable that if a slave outlived his keep, his own master could put him down like any aged or injured horse or dog.

With his hair cropped close to his head and typically clad in undyed wool, the thrall, as he was known, was an object of such contempt that it was a legal offense in some regions of Norway to libel a free man by calling him a slave. Even in the exercise of his own minimal legal rights, the slave was degraded: thus a Norwegian law stipulated that if a thrall found another man in bed with his wife, his only recourse was "to go to the brook and take a bucket full of water and throw it over them." In the poem *Rigspula*, the sons of a slave family were given such names as Coarse, Cleg, Foul, Lump, Thickard and Laggard; among the daughters were She-lump, Clump, Crane-shank, Tatter-coat, Beaked-nose and Thicklegs. As for the father: "rough were his hands/with wrinkled skin,/with knuckles knotty and fingers thick;/his face was ugly,/his back was humpy,/his heels were long."

The Norse sagas are filled with references to slavery, as are the chronicles of churchmen. Throughout the Ninth Century, Irish prisoners were transported "over the broad green sea" to the centers of Viking slave trade such as Hedeby, and Magdeburg to the south. In 837, recounted a poet, Walcheren at the mouth of the Scheldt was sacked, and "many women were led away captive." When raiders from Denmark struck France some years later, a scribe wrote: "They seize the country people, bind them and send them across the sea." In 870, the Frankish Archbishop Rimbert was at Hedeby, where he was so moved by the sight of Christian slaves that he sold his church vessels to buy their freedom. Once he saw a miserable troop filing by in chains, under armed guard. Some of the wretches cried out that they were Christians, and one woman sang psalms to show that she was a nun. For her freedom, Rimbert traded his horse and saddle.

The loathsome institution was no respecter of rank. Even Norway's Olaf Tryggvason, great-grandson of Harald Fairhair and himself one of the most feared of Viking kings around the turn of the millennium, spent his boyhood in slavery. After his father, King Tryggvi Olafsson, was overthrown and killed, Olaf's mother Astrid attempted to flee with her

The great unicorn horn of plenty

The greatest swindle ever perpetrated by the Vikings when they pushed into far northern waters was their sale of the long, whorled tusk of a small arctic mammal called the narwhal as the horn of a unicorn, wondrous beast of age-old legend. For men who believed in magic, and for whom the line between fact and fable was often obscured, it was not difficult to believe that such a horn possessed marvelous powers.

The unicorn first appears in the ancient lore of India and the Near East. In the Fourth Century B.C., the Greek Ctesias described it as a white horselike creature with a purple head and blue eyes. On its head was a long horn that was red at the top, black in the middle and white at the base. He went on to note that the creature was "exceedingly swift and powerful."

But this splendid animal, the ancients believed, was especially difficult to capture. According to a Sixth Century writer, when "it finds itself pursued and in danger of capture, it throws itself from a precipice and turns so aptly in falling that it receives all the

shock upon the horn and so escapes safe and sound."

But a clever hunter could dupe the unicorn. According to legend, one tactic was for the hunter to stand in front of a tree and taunt the unicorn until it charged him, horn lowered. At the last instant the hunter would step aside; the angry animal would drive its horn into the tree, thereby rendering itself helpless. Another method, recorded by Benedictine Abbess Hildegard in 1156, was to take advantage of the unicorns' susceptibility to beautiful virgins. When such a maiden was stationed in its path, a unicorn would prance up and lay its head in her lap, only to have it whacked off by a hunter hiding nearby.

However the unicorn met its end, the horn, in powder form, was presumed to be an aphrodisiac, an antidote for poisons, a cure for epilepsy and a remedy for diarrhea. A piece of the horn could be used to detect poison in food or to purify water. And the cunning Viking traders found eager buyers for all the unicorn horns they could get—from the arctic narwhal.

With head held high, the legendary unicorn proudly displays its horn in this 17th Century illustration from The Historie of Foure-Footed Beasts. The unicorn was just as formidable as it appeared, according to early scholars, who averred that it had "the harshest and most contentious voice" and was a "mortal enemy to the elephant."

baby boy to the realm of the Rus, where her brother Sigurd held high power. Halfway across the Baltic, they were beset and taken by pirates, who imprisoned the fair Astrid and sold the three-year-old Olaf into slavery "for a stout and good ram." Six years later his uncle Sigurd, on business in Estonia, saw a handsome lad in a marketplace, asked who he was—and ransomed Olaf.

A sequel to the story of Olaf's liberation from slavery demonstrates the equivocal relationship that existed between a master and even the most trusted of his thralls. In 995, after a career that had brought him fame and fortune as a Viking raider, Olaf returned to his homeland to lay claim to the throne that had been wrested from his father. The usurper, Earl Hakon Sigurdarsson, was swiftly forced into flight, accompanied only by his slave Kark.

They had been born on the same day, these two, and had gone through life together, Kark sleeping at the foot of his master's bed in peacetime and carrying his arms into war. Now, as they found final refuge in a pigsty, they heard Olaf loudly proclaiming that he would richly reward the man who found and killed the earl. At that, Kark's face flushed with greed, then blanched in fear of the consequences of the act he had in mind. "Why are you so pale?" Hakon demanded. "And now again as black as earth? You don't intend to betray me?"

Kark gave his word that he had no such idea in mind. As the terrible night passed, the two men crouched alone in their foul hiding place and, by the light of a flickering candle, stared at each other in mutual fear and distrust—until, toward daybreak, Earl Hakon Sigurdarsson slipped into sleep. Thereupon, without an instant's hesitation, Kark slit his master's throat.

Alas, when Kark presented Hakon's head to Olaf and claimed the reward, he found the great Viking to be most ungrateful. Although—or perhaps because—he had been a slave himself, Olaf knew that the structure of Viking society could not withstand the forgiving of a slave who lifted his hand against his master. He immediately ordered that Kark's head be chopped off.

The Vikings would take slaves wherever they found them. But their primary source of supply was in the East, where numberless tribes of Slavs—the name from which the word slave was derived—were still living in the Stone Age and were easy prey for the raiding parties that swooped down on them in forest or steppe and led them away in long fettered lines.

The role of the slave in the courts of Viking rulers in the far reaches of their Russian domains was not unlike that of the slaves in the Caliphate of Baghdad or in the sheikdoms of Araby. In 922 a Moslem trader by the name of Ibn Fadlan, who was probably on a slave-buying expedition himself at the time, described one such court of the Volga Rus, as the Russian Vikings were known: "It is customary for the king of the Rus to have a bodyguard in his castle of 400 reliable men willing to die for him. Each of these has a slave girl to wait on him, wash him and serve him, and another to sleep with. These 400 sit below the royal throne, a large and bejeweled platform that also accommodates the 40 slave girls of his harem. The King frequently has public intercourse with one of these."

As was the custom of the day, these chattels accompanied their master in death with elaborate ceremony. As Ibn Fadlan recounted the ritual: "When a chieftain among them has died, his family demands of his slave women and servants: 'Which of you wishes to die with him?' Then one of them says, 'I do'; and having said that the person concerned is forced to do so, and no backing out is possible."

In one case the Arab traveler relates, the doomed slave girl's attendants kept her generously primed with *nabid*—probably a strong Scandinavian beer—and before long she was moving in a drugged trance from tent to tent throughout the encampment: "And the owner of each tent had sexual intercourse with her, saying, 'Tell your master I did this out of love for him.'"

After 10 days of this, the deceased Viking was finally placed on a pyre beneath a tent aboard a small ship that had been specially constructed for the ceremony. Then arrived a crone, called the Angel of Death, who was to preside over the proceedings. The slave girl was given a beaker of *nabid*, then another. "But the old woman told her to hurry," recounted the Arab trader, "and drink up and enter the tent, where her master was. When I looked at her she seemed completely bewildered. She wanted to enter the tent and she put her head between it and the ship. There the woman took her head and managed to get it inside the tent, and the woman herself followed.

"Then the men began to beat the shields with wooden sticks, to deaden her shouts so that the other girls would not become afraid and shrink from dying with their masters. Six men entered the tent and all of them had intercourse with her. Thereafter they laid her by the side of her dead master. Two held her hands and two her feet, and the woman called the Angel of Death put a cord round the girl's neck, doubled with an end at each side, and gave it to two men to pull. Then she advanced holding a small dagger with a broad blade and began to plunge it between the girl's ribs to and fro while the two men choked her."

Thus the slave girl followed her master into death—where she was doubtless better off than in life.

Wherever they traveled, with whatever goods and chattels, the Vikings, at least in the early years, were rude and crude customers, utterly insensible to the niceties of mercantile conduct, ever ready to enforce a price or bring about a bargain at the point of a sword. As time went on, Viking conduct in the marketplace became more sophisticated. By the 13th Century, the unknown author of a Norwegian work called the *King's Mirror* could even offer an informal code for prudent and ethical merchants' behavior.

"When you are in a market town," advised the *King's Mirror*, "or wherever you are, be polite and agreeable; then you will secure the friendship of all good men. If you are unacquainted with the traffic of the town, observe carefully how those who are reputed to be the best and most prominent merchants conduct their business. You must also be careful to examine the wares that you buy before the purchase is finally made to make sure that they are sound and flawless. And whenever you make a purchase, call in a few trusty men to serve as witnesses as to how the bargain was made.

"You should keep occupied with your business till breakfast or, if necessity demands it, till midday. After the meal you may either take a nap or stroll around a little while to pass the time and to see what other good merchants are employed with, or whether any new wares that you ought to buy have come to the borough. On returning to your lodgings examine your wares, lest they suffer damage after coming into your hands. If they are found to be injured and you are about to dispose of them, do not conceal the flaws from the purchaser; show him what the defects are and make such a bargain; then you cannot be called a deceiver. Also put a good price on your wares, though not too high, and yet very near what you can see be obtained; then you cannot be called a cheat."

In journeys abroad, said the *King's Mirror*, the "man who is to be a trader will have to brave many perils." Why should he wish to take such risks? To the author, the answer lay "in man's threefold nature. One motive is fame and rivalry, for it is in the nature of man to seek a place where great dangers may be met and thus to win fame. A second motive is curiosity, for it is also in man's nature to wish to see and experience the things that he has heard about, and thus to learn whether the facts are as told or not. The third is desire for gain; for men seek wealth wherever they have heard that gain is to be gotten, though, on the other hand, there may be great dangers too."

In so saying, the writer with a merchant's mind and a Viking's heart was referring specifically to the great Norse movement across the North Atlantic to Iceland, Greenland and beyond.

Grotesque heads decorate the four corners of this elaborately carved horse-drawn wooden sledge that served as winter transportation for people and trade goods. The headposts were protection against evil spirits and served as holds for the ties that secured the box to its runners; in summer the detachable body was affixed to a wheeled frame and became a carriage.

Chapter 5

Bold pioneers in a land of ice and fire

*Surrounded by snarling sea monsters and jagged ice packs,
Iceland's wrinkled fjords and volcanic uplands at first glance seem
inhospitable. Yet this 16th Century Dutch engraving contains a
profusion of symbols: a fishery (left) and pasturage (center), plus
some 40 Viking settlements in the "land of fire and ice."*

is name was Naddod and, for exploits unrecorded but doubtless rude, he was known as a *vikingr mikill*—a "Viking of note." By about 860 A.D., however, his violent presence was no longer welcome in his native Norway and, in the words of a chronicler, Naddod with a few companions "went off to make a home for himself in the Faroes for the good reason that he had nowhere else where he would be safe."

Thanks partly to Naddod, the barren, wind-swept Faroe Islands northwest of the Shetlands would one day become vitally important as a navigational turnoff point for Viking voyages of exploration and settlement in faraway lands. But now the tiny chain served only as a lair for others of Naddod's ilk, Norse marauders who occupied their energies raiding Scotland and Ireland to the southeast.

On the way to this place of refuge, Naddod was caught by a terrible storm and, though his square-cut sail could ordinarily hold the ship's curved prow on a desired heading, it was no match for a live North Atlantic gale. Naddod was blown far off course—as it turned out, some 240 miles northwest of the Faroes. His landfall came on a forbidding coast, riven by swollen rivers and dominated by ice-encrusted mountains. Naddod and his men climbed to a summit and gazed out at the contorted wasteland for some indication of human habitation. But "they saw never a sign," reports the chronicler. As they sailed away, shaping a course to the Faroes, heavy snow began to fall, leading Naddod to call the place Snowland.

And that is all the chronicler has to say about Naddod, the exiled Viking—presumably because he did nothing further of note.

At about the same time and by similar accident, another Norse rover reached that same hostile shore. He was a Swede named Gardar Svavarsson, who was sailing for the Hebrides when a storm struck him in Pentland Firth, the narrow sea passage between the Orkneys and the mainland of Scotland. The storm carried him far westward to a hook-shaped promontory, since become known as the East Horn, about 50 miles south of Naddod's landfall.

But unlike Naddod, Gardar and his crew did not, after making a brief inspection, turn back. Whether seeking safe shelter or driven by the compulsions of a true explorer, Gardar steered southwest, hugging a ragged coastline and passing a wall of ice looming 5,000 feet high and stretching more than 50 miles from east to west at the terminus of a great glacier. He groped along the southern shore, virtually treeless, harborless and desolate. He came within sight of twin volcanoes, monsters that breathed smoke and flame, causing the earth to tremble and the sea to roil, siring vast lava fields where thousands of snow-white sea birds nested amid the hardened black and twisted rock forms. Bearing northwest with the curve of the coast, Gardar threaded between the mainland and a group of islands whose dark, brooding cliffs would within a few years take morbid place in the region's lore.

Rounding a peninsula that extended due west 30 miles from the mainland, Gardar passed by the largest and best harbor in all the land. He may not even have seen it, for it was later to be named Reykjavik—meaning

"Smoky Bay"—and it was often misted over by the vapors from a witch's brew of surrounding geysers, steaming springs and boiling mudholes.

Gardar pointed his prow to the northwest and sailed across a bay 60 miles wide, its waters gleaming in reflection of the surrounding, snow-crowned mountains. The little Viking vessel crossed and perhaps prowled into the mouth of a vast fjord, where the profusion of rocky islets and swirling currents reminded Gardar of home. The ship then clawed around the contorted fingers of a northwest peninsula, and sailed back east along a relatively benign shoreline, broken by fjords that offered haven and by valleys green with grass.

Gardar passed them all by. Summer was ending and the hour was fast approaching when he must beach his ship for winter. Yet evidently within him was an urge to press on, to see what lay around the next bend, to explore beyond the next promontory. At last, arctic blasts told him he must stop—at one of the least hospitable places along the northern coast. This was to be known as Skjalfandi, or the "Trembler," for its proximity to a volcanic area. There, on a cliff above a bay that lay open to arctic ice floes, Gardar built a hut for himself and his weary crew.

Winter can only have been wretched for these Viking explorers. The chronicles, perhaps mercifully, do not go into it. In any case, at the first sign of a fair spring breeze, Gardar put back to sea, departing so hastily that he failed to search for and find a crew member named Nattfari, along with a slave and a bondwoman who had become separated from the main party. (Somehow Nattfari survived, for his name is mentioned in the chronicles as an early settler; what befell the other two is unknown.) Gardar now sailed northeast around the Melrakkasletta headlands, then generally south and east back to his starting point at the East Horn. He had followed a coastline that, with its countless deep indentations, measured no fewer than 3,700 miles. Gardar apparently liked some of what he had seen—at least to the point of naming the vast, strange island he had explored after himself: Gardarsholm.

In such Scandinavian trading towns as Hedeby, Birka and Skiringssal, in the expatriate Viking communities of Scotland and Ireland, at raiding bases in the Orkneys, Shetlands and Faroes, wherever Norsemen gathered to boast of high adventure, word of the discoveries of Naddod and Gardar spread. Before long, possibly within a year or two, another seafarer set forth. Like Naddod, Floki Vilgerdarson was a Norwegian *vikingr mikill*. Unlike either Naddod or Gardar, Floki purposely set his red-and-white-striped sail for the new-found western island—evidently intending to settle there, for he had loaded cattle and family aboard his ship.

Floki's route set a pattern for future voyages: sailing from southwest Norway, he landed first at the Shetlands (where, under circumstances now unknown, a daughter drowned), then steered west and slightly north for nearly 200 miles to the Faroes (where another daughter was married). These stops behind him, Floki headed for the island of ice and fire, nearly 240 miles to the northwest. Perhaps because Naddod and Gardar had been understandably fuzzy about directions, Floki had on board some navigational aids once embarked by the Biblical Noah: three birds. In this case they were large ravens and, when released from their

Norway's King Harald Fairhair, shown here at left shaking hands in a rare moment of cordiality with the Danish chieftain Guthrum, ruled his domain with such a heavy hand and marble heart that many of his subjects fled to Iceland and other remote places. During the summer Harald would entertain himself by combing the coastal islands in search of fugitive Vikings who, as the sagas relate, "took flight straight out into the open ocean when they saw him coming."

cages, they could be seen in silhouette against the pale sky and followed for miles as they flew presumably toward the nearest land.

Before departing, Floki had taken the precaution of hallowing his blackbirds by making a great sacrifice—the accounts do not relate whether man or beast—to the gods so that they would smile on his winged guides. Now, out of sight of the Faroes, Floki uncaged his first raven, which soared into the sky, took its sightings and set a straight course back to the Faroes. Undaunted, Floki sailed on, released the second raven and watched bemusedly as it flapped about in a few circles, then landed on the ship. Onward forged Floki, his faith still in the birds. And his trust was amply rewarded: the third raven flew west, leading Floki—henceforth to be known as Raven Floki—to the East Horn of the western island at almost the same spot where Gardar the Swede had begun his circumnavigation.

Raven Floki, his men, his cattle and what remained of his family followed Gardar's route around the island, marveling at the same sights, until they came to a great fjord in the northwest, later to be called Breida-fjord. There they decided to settle.

Alas, Raven Floki was a better sailor than a settler. The fjord was alive with salmon and cod and seal, the grass grew lush along its shores and, while his cattle grew fat, Raven Floki fished and hunted to his heart's content—all the while neglecting to put up hay for winter. As a result of his negligence, his livestock perished before spring. Raven Floki bitterly blamed the land for his own improvidence. Then he packed up, and late that second summer he sailed for Norway. But dreadful southwesterly gales howled across the waters for much of the time, and Raven Floki could not get around the most southerly headland. He and his men had to spend another awful winter shivering in a primitive camp. Not until the next summer did they pass the guardian headland and reach home.

Although they had all endured the same hardships, not all Floki's followers shared their leader's negative feelings. One of them, a man named Thorolf, told of butter dripping from every blade of the island's grass. For that obvious embroidery on the fabric of truth, he won a derisive nickname—Thorolf Butter. Precisely what Thorolf meant remains a mystery. He may have been talking about the exceedingly heavy dew at night caused in subarctic lands by rapid cooling and high humidity. Or he may, in a flight of fancy, have been alluding to the lush grass from which cows would give rich milk for cheese and butter.

In any event, Raven Floki had the last word. Out of his anger, he gave to the island the name it still possesses: Iceland.

Naddod the Norwegian, Gardar the Swede and Raven Floki were but the fore edge of the Norse wave that within a flick of historic time would break over Iceland. The Vikings sailed to Iceland not as conquerors but as settlers. They sought not booty but farmland and goods with which to trade. To land-hungry Norwegians, cramped in their little patches of real estate, the call of the new country, where vast stretches of land were open for the taking, must have seemed every bit as alluring as any treasure that might be snatched by force. As added inducement to emigration, Norway's King Harald Fairhair was consolidating his power with a strong hand and, in the words of an Icelandic saga, "He made everyone do one thing or the other: become his retainers or quit the country."

Within a scant 60 years after the first voyages, Iceland's population reached 20,000, and after another century, 60,000. Iceland drew its first settlers most heavily from the long Norwegian littoral between Agdir and southern Halogaland, especially from the areas around Sogn, Hordaland and Rogaland in the southwest. These were the places of greatest resistance to the all-grasping rule of King Harald Fairhair, and these were the places where his fist descended most heavily. In later years, even under benign rulers, Norwegians from throughout the land, goaded by the prospect of a brighter future, gathered their belongings and headed for Iceland.

It was only natural that life in the new colony should find its genesis in the savage and senseless ways of the old lands. Among the first permanent settlers in the late 860s were two Norwegian foster brothers, Ingolf Arnarson and Hjorleif Hrodmarsson, who might never have considered the place had they not engaged in a feud over a woman with the sons of the powerful Earl Atli the Slender of Gaular. When the fighting had ended, two of the noble's sons were dead. Forced to forfeit most of their estates for blood money, Ingolf and Hjorleif judiciously decided to leave Norway. They used their remaining assets to outfit a ship and, according to the *Landnamabok,* the "Book of Settlements," a 12th Century work that named the earliest settlers and gave details of their lives, "set off to find that land Raven Floki had discovered—the one called Iceland."

Mixing caution with boldness in typical Viking fashion, the foster brothers made their first voyage a reconnaissance. Arriving at Iceland's East Horn, they swung down to the southern coast and, in the close sailing the Vikings did best, threaded through sand reefs into the protected waters of the Alptafjord, where they spent the winter scouting. Returning to Norway, Ingolf took charge of winding up their affairs while Hjorleif, to raise more capital, went a-Viking in Ireland. There he took 10 Irish warriors as slaves, and seized enough loot to acquire a second ship and provision the two.

Each at the helm of his own ship, Ingolf and Hjorleif once more cruised the southern coast of Iceland, where Ingolf, according to ancient custom, threw into the sea the pillars, adorned by carvings and dedicated to Thor, of his high seat at home. Where Thor allowed the current to carry the pillars ashore, Ingolf vowed he would make his permanent home. The pillars drifted rapidly westward and Ingolf, in full faith that he would find them in his own good time, went directly ashore. He probably wintered near Oraefi, where, in one of Iceland's many dramatic contrasts, long swathes of grassland intrude between the outstretched fingers of a great glacier.

As for Hjorleif, either swept by the same current that had taken Ingolf's pillars or wishing to strike out on his own, he headed west and landed some 70 miles down the coast, where he built a house, the ruins of which still stand on the seaward edge of black volcanic sands. When spring arrived, he diligently set about clearing and planting his land, but he soon ran into a snag: he had only one ox to pull his plow. Striking upon a

A saintly passage to a paradise far away

The first bold voyagers to cross the North Atlantic may not have been Vikings but Irish monks sworn to wander the world for Christ. Possibly, St. Brendan and others sailed to Iceland as early as the Sixth Century, and perhaps even to North America.

Ancient Irish literature abounds in such tales. But St. Brendan's story is set in such a sea of whimsy that scholars cannot sort fact from fancy.

St. Brendan was born in the late Fifth Century near Tralee, County Kerry. He lived a fruitful life, and by age 70 he had founded four monasteries and had sailed around the British Isles on religious missions. Then, say the tales, he heard of a voyage by the son of a fellow abbot across the ocean to the "Promised Land of the Saints."

Undaunted by age, St. Brendan and a crew of 18 tonsured monks set sail for this glorious destination in a leatherhulled Irish *curragh*, which, according to one story, was "a very light little vessel, ribbed and sided with wood and covered with oak-tanned hides and caulked with ox tallow."

The adventures that followed were reminiscent of Homer's *Odyssey*: St. Brendan encountered a comic whale and an island of birds chanting orisons; he sailed through ice floes and escaped monsters; passing a volcanic island, he was frightened by a lavahurling devil; until at last he reached the Promised Land.

After exploring this earthly paradise, St. Brendan returned to Ireland. Where paradise was remains a mystery. But in the Ninth Century, Vikings found Irish monks living in Iceland as hermits, and later reported the monks in a place the sagas call "Ireland the Great" that "lies away west in the ocean nigh to Vinland."

The friendly whale Jasconius coils himself around St. Brendan's skin boat as the venturesome prelate and his crew waft across the western Atlantic to new lands. "They sailed in this manner for 14 days," insists this wonderfully illustrated 15th Century German account. At one point, before releasing them, the prankish cetacean permitted the monks to dine alfresco on his back.

St. Brendan's adventure begins when the bold abbot, always grasping his shepherd's crook, selects a crew of like-minded monks. The German account says: "All returned with him but one who was taken unto paradise and another who was taken by the devil"—a lost soul who apparently stole a silver necklace from a castle discovered on their first landfall.

Accosted by a fire-breathing dragon labeled drache, *St. Brendan successfully implores God to send "a large animal resembling a buck that burned like fire and threw the dragon into the air."*

Reaching paradise, St. Brendan, records the German text, finds "the ground golden and green from many precious stones. They saw the most beautiful building with walls of gold and columns of carbuncle; the roof was of peacock feathers, and a fountain flowed rivers of milk and honey, wine and oil."

Threatened by a devil brandishing lava on a volcanic isle, St.
Brendan is told: "If I dared before God, I could have you all killed
and thrown into this fiery mass in revenge for the souls lost to
me by your prayers." But the power of prayer carried St. Brendan
safely through his journey and into the pages of history.

simple solution to the problem, he yoked his Irish slaves—those whom he had seized during his last expedition—along with the animal. The men took this indignity with ill grace, complaining bitterly and promising themselves revenge.

When they were out of Hjorleif's sight, they killed the ox and blamed the deed on a forest bear. Hjorleif was too new to the land to know that, except for an occasional polar bear brought down on an arctic floe, there were no such beasts in Iceland. He and his followers went beating the birchwoods in pursuit of the nonexistent attacker. The slaves, in turn, tracked the scattered trackers, fell on them separately and murdered them all. Thereupon the Irishmen seized all the Viking women, collected all the goods they could carry, loaded everything into a skiff and rowed for safety to some offshore islands—the same brooding islands that Gardar the Swede had noticed during his circumnavigation.

Ingolf, meanwhile, had sent men down the coast to search for his pillars. In due course, they came upon the gruesome scene of the Hjorleif slaughter, and raced frantically back to report to their leader. In a fury of vengeance, Ingolf descended on the place, soon found the Irish hideaway in the offshore isles, butchered some of the slaves and drove the rest to a horrible death over the cliffs. The little island group has ever since been known as the Vestmannaeyjar, meaning West-Man Islands, because the Irish were called by the Norwegians the men of the West.

Duty done, Ingolf spent his second winter at Hjorleif's abandoned place, then continued west in quest of the pillars. At the Olfus River, dividing line between a pleasant grassland area and the hellish lava fields of the Reykjanes promontory, he halted, sending two thralls ahead to continue the search for the pillars. By some fantastic stroke of luck, the seat posts were actually found—in perhaps the least inviting place in all Iceland, a moonscape of volcanic dust and craters at the head of a fog-shrouded bay. "Great grief is ours," moaned one of the men, "to have passed through such excellent country and now have to live on this Godforsaken cape." But Ingolf was true to Thor—he built his house where the pillars were found. And Thor had evidently led him well: with its superb harbor, Reykjavik eventually became the capital of Iceland, the center of Icelandic commercial and cultural life.

For his settlement, according to the *Landnamabok*, Ingolf claimed the territory "between the Olfus River and Hvalfjord west of Brynjudalsa, and between there and Oxara, and the whole of the land projecting west." Here indeed was a colossal holding—some 1,000 square miles. Ingolf remained there the rest of his days, hunting, farming and raising livestock with what must have been considerable success. For he fathered a large brood that became one of Iceland's premier dynasties, active and powerful in every phase of life from religion and trade to politics.

Both Icelandic literature and the evidence from ancient Icelandic graves indicate that something like 85 per cent of the pioneer-settlers were Norwegians like Ingolf. Of the early names recorded in the *Landnamabok*, only a few were Swedish or Danish, probably because these Viking peoples did not suffer from the tyranny endured by the Norwegians. But the book contains large numbers of Celtic or celticized names, presumably because of the intermarriage between Norwegians and Irish-

Snarling menacingly, a carved oaken dragon head sits atop its magnificently crafted neck, which is still tenoned at the bottom, where it was probably joined to the stempost of a Norse warship. Such elaborate bow ornaments were intended not only to terrify the raiders' victims but also to guard against evil spirits at sea.

men and Scots. In addition, the settlers brought along large numbers of Celtic slaves, by whom they often fathered children. And so there soon developed a strong strain of mixed Norse-Celtic blood in the veins of the early inhabitants of Iceland.

Wherever these first settlers set out from, they all endured discomfort and danger during the journey to Iceland. Yet seafaring was so much a part of everyday Viking life, storms were so commonplace in the North Atlantic and death at sea so much to be taken for granted that the sagas treated the voyage as if it were no more than a matter of crossing a fjord. Thus, in its entirety, the *Landnamabok* account of what must have been a truly spectacular shipwreck: "On Good Friday itself a merchant ship was driven ashore under Eyjafjall, spun into the air, 54-oared vessel as she was, and dashed down bottom up."

Still, archeological evidence and other scholarship have filled many of the gaps. Leaving behind their sleek and deadly longships, the Viking settlers traveled to Iceland in their ship-of-all-work, the knarr, which they fondly called the "goat of the sea" for her ability to bound over the waves. Absent from the prows were the monstrous figureheads whose main purpose was to instill dread. When the Icelanders got around to drawing a legal code, one of the first laws adopted forbade approaching land "with gaping heads and yawning jaws, so that the spirits of the land grow frightened of them."

During a good 24-hour day of fresh breezes, a smartly crewed knarr could cover upward of 150 miles, for an average of better than five knots. Thus it was often possible to make the crossing from Norway in five or six days. One saga reported a crossing from More, Norway, to western Iceland, a distance of 730 nautical miles, in four days and four nights—which averages out to an impressive 7.5 knots. A voyage from the Faroes might take as little as two days and two nights.

Nevertheless, the Vikings were braving some of the world's most difficult waters, with only rudimentary navigational instructions. It was assumed that any Viking seafarer could reach the Faroes. With those islands as a landmark, it was simple enough—even with the primitive Norse devices for calculating direction—to steer northwest until Iceland hove into sight. But all of this was far more easily said than done. Fierce storms in the North Atlantic often blew the Iceland-bound emigrants far off course—or crushed their craft to splinters. Nor was the sight of Iceland any assurance of a safe landfall at journey's end. Still more perils attended the Vikings as they felt their way through Iceland's wicked reefs and shifting sandbars, and probed into rocky fjords in their quest for the sight and sweet scent of grass on which to make their claims and husband their animals.

Among the most renowned settlers was a great matriarch named Aud the Deep Minded, whose tale in the *Laxdaela Saga* speaks for Viking character and fortitude, and for the bountiful haven the Vikings found in Iceland. Aud was the daughter of Ketil Flatnose, a mighty Norwegian who had fled with his family from Harald Fairhair and had established dominance over the Hebrides. Her son, Thorstein the Red, ruled a vast domain in Scotland in alliance with a Viking earl named Sigurd, and Aud might not have considered Iceland had not bizarre calamity struck.

In the course of the incessant battles of the day, Sigurd challenged a Scottish earl, known to the Vikings as Melbrikta Tusk (because he had one huge protruding tooth), to combat with 40 horses on each side. With typical Viking guile, Sigurd put two men on each horse, overwhelmed the enemy, cut off Melbrikta's head and hung it from his saddle bows. But then as he galloped on in the pride of victory, the dead man's tooth pierced his calf. Before long, the wound festered and he died.

Thorstein attempted to go it alone, and for a time was victorious over the Scots, gaining a treaty of peace with his enemies. But the Scots did not honor the treaty for long. One day they descended on Thorstein at Caithness and there, catching him off guard, slew the Viking chieftain.

Deprived of her protectors, Aud seemed at the mercy of her enemies. They encircled her late son's domain in Caithness and were already savoring the joys of dividing the treasure when she slipped through their fingers. She had had a ship built in secrecy in a forest by the sea. While her foes slumbered, she launched it on a dark night and loaded it with all her valuables and set sail with her grandchildren and an armed band of faithful followers. "It is generally thought," says the Laxdaela Saga, "that it would be hard to find another example of a woman escaping from such hazards with so much wealth and such a large retinue. From this it can be seen what a paragon among women she was."

Aud sailed off to the northern seas. In the Orkneys she married off one of her granddaughters to the earl who ruled the isles; in the Faroes she married off another to a rich landowner. But she felt cramped in both places, and now she listened to news of the empty lands in Iceland waiting for a bold hand to seize them. Two of her brothers had already gone there, and the indomitable matriarch now followed them, sailing another 240 miles across the storm-tossed ocean.

It was a harrowing voyage, and a still rougher arrival: her ship struck a reef and sank. But she scrambled safely to shore with her remaining grandchildren, 20 retainers and a number of slaves, and most of her precious and by now well-traveled goods. She found her way to the farmhouse of one brother, Helgi, and he offered to put her up—but told her he could take only nine of her companions. She called him a mean-minded, misbegotten disgrace to the family, turned on her heel and stalked out of the house. Then she went over the narrow rocky trails to her other brother, Bjorn, and he invited her to stay with all her companions, "for," says the Laxdaela Saga, "he knew his sister's nature." She remained with him for a while, then she went exploring the empty lands to the west, sailing from one headland to another, laying claim to every river valley that struck her fancy and lighting ritual bonfires to establish her ownership.

The fertile territories she had surveyed and laid claim to were immense—"all valley lands between Dogurdara and Skraumuhlaupsa," records the saga, a tract of some 180 square miles. She parceled this land out on a lavish scale to her faithful companions and to her slaves, showing particular favor to a Scottish nobleman whom her son had captured years before and whom she now set free. When she married off one of her last granddaughters, she gave her a whole river valley as dowry.

Upon the coming of age of her dear departed Thorstein's youngest son, a boy named Olaf, she chose a wife for him and gave a great feast. Families of pioneers came from great distances at her invitation. She got up late that day, saw to it that prodigious quantities of ale were poured out to the guests, then stumped off to bed, stout and stately. In the morning, her grandson found her sitting bolt upright in bed, quite dead, a matriarch to the last.

In the days of the pioneers like Aud, land was free for the asking. As private practice or as public policy, this was profligate, and it could only lead to quarrels and killings. With the passage of time and the arrival of more and more Norsemen competing for space, strict limits had to be imposed. It was finally decreed that a man could claim only so much ground as he could travel around on foot in a single day while carrying a lighted torch. The stipulations in the new rule for a woman provided that she could lay claim to only such territory as she could cover in a day—while leading a two-year-old cow.

Still, those early Icelanders may perhaps be forgiven for thinking there was more than enough land for everyone. Iceland was a very large island: 325 miles at its longest from east to west, 185 miles at its widest from north to south, 39,758 square miles in its land area. Yet that mass was deceiving: fully one eighth of the land was overlaid by lava beds, another one eighth by glaciers, and much of the rest by volcanic mountains, lifeless sands, rock-littered moraines and other topographic waste. Thus, of the entire area, less than 7,000 square miles was habitable, much less arable.

Yet along the sea's edge, on the flanks of the fjords thrusting deep into the interior, even on the lower slopes of the mountains, grew the precious grass that meant life for the Icelanders. Here, too, the settlers could cultivate grains. There was a rolling green-and-gold beauty to these lands that could swell the heart of even the most hardheaded and pragmatic of Icelanders. It was in expression of his love for his farmstead that Gunnar of Hlidarendi, hero of one of the most beautiful of all Icelandic literary works, Njals Saga, chose death over life. Involved in one blood feud after another, Gunnar was finally condemned to exile for his slayings. As he rode away from his farms, his horse stumbled and turned, and Gunnar looked back at the grassy hills above his farm. "Fair is the slope," he said, "and never has it seemed more fair to me, the cornfields pale and the meadows mowed. I shall ride back home and not leave it." He returned in full knowledge that his enemies would soon kill him. And so they did in an overwhelming attack—but only after his wife, Hallgerd, a mean, vengeful woman, had refused him a lock of her hair to twist into his broken bowstring. She had never forgiven the one and only time he had slapped her, in a fit of anger many years before.

On the grass and grains, Icelandic livestock not only survived but evidently prospered. The sagas tell of a farmer who set about tallying his sheep, finally tired of counting and stopped at 2,400. Another, while exploring for a new homestead, "put a couple of pigs ashore, a boar by the name of Solvi and a sow, and when they were found three years later in Solvadal"—Solvi's Valley—"all told there were 70 of them."

The grass, roots and all, contributed the main building material, sod,

A rough-and-ready rule of law

The Vikings of Iceland were remarkable not only for the force of will with which they wrested a living from their desolate island, but also for the laws by which they governed themselves. These laws were based on a Norwegian code, as adjusted to meet the needs of the Icelanders.

It is no surprise that among such a volatile people sharing so little arable land, 10 of the code's 12 main sections dealt with civil and criminal law. A free man convicted of theft for the first time might only be fined or flogged, but a slave in similar circumstances might be mutilated. An unregenerate thief could be hanged or outlawed, and a murderer faced the same fate.

Another section of the law dealt with a favorite Viking sport—horsefighting, in which two trained stallions were pitted against each other. The law prescribed that "Wherever men goad a man's horse to fight without his leave, compensation shall be paid to the owner of the horse for what was done out of enmity and malice."

The remaining two sections of the code dealt with maritime affairs—the most important matters to the seagirt Icelanders. One section covered the division of valuable flotsam washed ashore, of the timbers and cargo from a wrecked vessel, or of the blubber and oil of a stranded whale. The other regulated seaborne trade and set forth the rights and duties of sailors.

For nearly two centuries, the laws were transmitted orally. The surviving written code, called the *Jonsbok*, after the man who brought this set of laws to Iceland, was probably inscribed around 1280, and even though the original document has since disappeared, some 200 splendidly illuminated copies, such as the 16th Century version shown here, remain as a record of Iceland's rule of law.

St. Olaf, Iceland's giver of laws, crushes the dragon of lawlessness beneath his feet.

Fish play in the waves ahead of a cargo vessel in a maritime section of the law code. The text refers to arrangements for freight handling.

for Icelandic homes. The forests of which the sagas sang were, in fact, coastal and streamside stands of puny, stunted, soft-wooded willow and birch. After a few years the land was denuded even of these, and it was a miraculous event, worthy of recording in the *Landnamabok,* when a tree more than 100 feet long drifted ashore. For in the whole of Iceland there was not a single oak or elm that could be used to make the massive roof beams of a traditional Norse long house. Iceland's ubiquitous rock, piles and piles of it in every field, was as useless for home building as the scrubby trees; it was volcanic in origin and thus soft and porous. But the Icelandic turf was quite another matter: it could be dug thick and solid with dirt, or cut carpet thin and tough.

The sod house developed by the Icelandic Vikings was generally convex, the slope of its sides gentle enough to deflect the wind and permit children and sheep to clamber to the rooftop to play or graze on the still-growing grass. It was anywhere between 40 and 100 feet in length, with turf walls three to six feet thick. The only windows were in the ends, simple holes papered over with translucent membrane from the birth sack of a calf. In the middle of the floor was a hearth, around which the women squatted while the men lorded it from benches. This hearth, fueled by dried sheep dung, was for warmth and socializing. Meals were usually cooked—the Vikings preferred boiled meat to roasted—elsewhere, in pits at the ends of the long central room. The floor was set at a higher level along the sides than in the center and was divided by stone or wooden partitions into sleeping compartments. As society developed in the 10th and 11th Centuries, other rooms—lobbies, kitchens, sculleries, storerooms—were added to the main hall. Nevertheless, even the best accommodations could only have been low, dark and smoky, and must have contributed much to the Vikings' natural ill temper.

The Icelandic sagas exalt Icelandic heroes. But even heroes must earn a living, and though they certainly did not beat their swords into plowshares, the settlers did take to the grinding agrarian life with a determination that knew no rank. "It was then the custom," says a saga, "for rich men's sons to put their hands to something useful." No one was surprised to see a highborn man tending his flocks or seeding and manuring his fields. The *Havamal,* a collection of sayings supposedly handed down by Odin, god of knowledge, is a veritable fount of homely pioneer observation and advice, with even a salting of humor. "Two goats and a poor-roofed cot," it advises, "are better than begging." "A man with few helpers must rise early and look to his work." "Out in the fields I gave my clothes to two scarecrows. They thought themselves champions once they had trappings. A naked man is shorn of confidence."

Prototypical of Iceland's pioneer farmers was Skallagrim Kveldulfsson, father of the great warrior-poet, Egil Skallagrimsson, and the hero of *Egil's Saga.* Skallagrim was a huge, dark, bald, ugly man of enormous strength. The saga recounts how once, needing an anvil for a smithy he had built, he dived into the waters of a fjord and came up with a boulder such as four ordinary men could not lift. He was also a man of towering temper, and it is not difficult to imagine the many and bloody fights that eventually resulted in his being forced to depart from Norway.

In selecting his property in Iceland, Skallagrim followed not the traditional pillars but rather the coffin of his father, who had died during the voyage. The coffin was tipped over the side at sea, and it came ashore at one of the most felicitous places in all Iceland, rich with grass and sweet water. In the days before limits, Skallagrim promptly claimed a 400-square-mile territory—"all the land," according to the saga, "bounded by the rivers right down to the sea."

As it turned out, Skallagrim was much more than a mere blood-lusting warrior. And now, as farmer, blacksmith, fisherman, boatbuilder and sailor, he was in his natural element. On his claim there was extensive marshland, teeming with wild fowl and broad pastures for livestock; farther inland the mountain streams were choked with salmon and trout. "Skallagrim," says the saga, "was a great man for hard work. He always had a good number of men working for him to get in all available provisions that might be useful for the household, for in the early stages they had little livestock, considering how many of them were there."

Because of the lack of suitable wooded land, most Icelanders perforce depended upon Norway for their boats. But Skallagrim was doubly fortunate. Not only was he a master shipwright, but he also found a treasure-trove of driftwood on part of his land. "So he built and ran another farm at Alptanes," continues the saga, "and from there his men went out fishing and seal hunting and collecting the eggs of wild fowl, for there was plenty of everything." His third farm he built by the sea in an even more favorable location for finding driftwood and whales.

"As Skallagrim's livestock grew in number, the animals started making for the mountains in the summer. He found a big difference in the livestock, which were much better and fatter when grazing up in the moorland, and above all in the sheep that wintered in the mountain valleys instead of being driven down. As a result, Skallagrim had a farm built near the mountains and ran it as a sheep farm. So the wealth of Skallagrim rested on a good many foundations."

From the wind-swept sheep runs of such farms as Skallagrim's came Iceland's principal export: wool. And within the fantasies of the later sagas lies a pleasant little story with a ring of truth. One summer in the 960s, an Icelandic ship arrived at Hardanger, Norway, with a cargo of great shaggy woven-wool cloaks—for which the traders could find no buyers. Their leader complained of his ill fortune to King Harald—a later and more benign Harald than the fearsome Fairhair of earlier history. And this Harald, being, says the saga, "very condescending, and full of fun," came with a large retinue to inspect the goods. "Will you give me a present of one of these gray cloaks?" he asked. "Willingly," replied the steersman. The King wrapped a cloak around his regal shoulders and departed—but only after every man in his following had purchased a gray cloak for himself. "In a few days," says the saga, "so many men came to buy cloaks that not half of them could be served with what they wanted." For having thus set a style—to the Icelanders' considerable profit—the King became known to history as Harald Graycloak.

Even as they turned their hand to the shear and the plow, the Icelanders remained a people of the sea. It had brought them to the new land, it sustained them there, and it was their commercial link to European markets. The cod and salmon that teemed in Iceland's waters were do-

Betraying its maker's pagan heritage, a 10th Century Icelandic silver amulet in the shape of a cross is fashioned with a dragon head at one end. Even after their mass conversion to Christianity in the year 1000, many Icelanders refused to abandon their favorite Norse gods and symbols. According to one Icelandic saga, merchants and soldiers cheerfully submitted to "provisional baptism," since they "had full communion with pagans and Christians alike yet could keep whatever faith was most agreeable."

mestic dietary staples and, when salted, a valuable export. Wild swans and other large aquatic birds provided their feathers for quill pens, and the down of Iceland's eider ducks filled the feather beds of Europe. Ivory from the tusks of Icelandic walruses sold at premium prices. Seals gave their skins, and every so often a floe-borne polar bear's luxuriant fur was worth a king's ransom.

There were huge and magnificent white falcons, the finest in all the world for hawking, a sport that was almost as popular as war with European kings and nobles of the day. And drifting ice packs sometimes crowded whales onto Iceland's beaches, providing the islanders with a feast and with oil for use both at home and in foreign trade.

Yet while the average Icelander was a hard-working farmer and trader, he was also the son of Vikings, with his ancestors' lust for wandering and adventure in his blood. From time to time, if his farm was in good hands—or even if it was not—he would sail off across the broad sea to the British Isles and Europe.

Many Icelanders simply headed in the direction of the nearest fight. Everyone knew and cherished the story of the Icelander named Thorstein, son of Hall, who in 1014 fought in the Viking army at the Battle of Clontarf, near Dublin. While all his comrades were in headlong flight, he stooped down calmly to tighten his bootlaces. The victorious Irish came upon him and asked why he was not fleeing with the rest. "Because," said he, "I can't get home tonight, since my home is out in Iceland." Admiring his coolness, they granted him his life.

And there was Halldor Snorrason, another Icelander, who had gone as far as man could go in Christendom to join the Varangian Guard, which protected the emperor in Constantinople. He formed a bluff and hearty friendship there with Harald Hardradi, commander of the Guard. When Harald later became king of Norway, Halldor stayed with him. But Harald as king was less of a friend, and he was also late in paying Halldor some money he owed him. The dauntless Icelander burst with drawn sword into the King's bedroom and forced the Queen to give him the solid-gold ring on her finger. Then he was down to the docks and off on his ship home to Iceland. The King's men in three longships tried to catch him but soon gave up the chase. Halldor lived comfortably on his farm, and though Harald often urged him to come back and promised him a higher position than anyone else in the land not nobly born, he always refused. Said Halldor, the crafty Viking, "I know his temper well enough: he'll keep his promise and hang me on the highest gallows."

There was a steady flow of tough, clever and self-reliant young men from Iceland to Norway. The Icelander Hrut Herjolfsson shared the bed of Gunnhild, the Queen Mother of Norway, and came back a rich man. Years later his nephew Olaf Peacock found the Queen just as amorous and just as generous. Olaf's son Kjartan made the voyage to Norway too, taking half shares in a cargo ship. One day he went swimming in the icy river off the port of Nidaros—now Trondheim—and noticed an especially strong swimmer in a group ahead of him. He decided to challenge him to a typically Viking sport.

As related in the *Laxdaela Saga*: "He made for this man and forced him underwater at once and held him there for a while before letting go of him. No sooner had they come to the surface than this man seized hold of Kjartan and pulled him down, and they stayed under for what seemed to Kjartan a very reasonable time. They surfaced for a second time, and still they exchanged no words. Then they went under for a third time and now they stayed down much longer than before. Kjartan was no longer sure how this game would end, and felt that he had never been in such a tight corner before. At last they came to the surface and swam ashore." As they stood on the bank, the man praised Kjartan for his strength and courage, and revealed that he was none other than the King of Norway, Olaf Tryggvason, the greatest Viking of his age. He gave Kjartan his richly embroidered cloak and showered him with favors afterward.

Olaf may have been moved by something more than admiration for the young man's strength and pluck, just as Harald Graycloak may have been interested in something more than setting a new style in men's fashions in his kingdom. As kings of Norway, they knew that most of the Icelandic colonists had come from their land, and they felt a natural urge to extend their dominion over Iceland, as they had gradually done over the Shetlands, the Orkneys, the Faroes.

But the Icelanders were far away, and at this time, in the flush of their success as colonists and as traders and as Vikings, they felt safe and self-reliant. They had no wish for any foreign master and desired to remain, as one of them put it, "free of kings and criminals." Moreover, on their outpost of civilization they had established a self-governing republic, something Europe had not seen since the early days of Rome.

Geography had dictated that Iceland be a land of isolated farmsteads — of many farmers separated from their neighbors by river, fjord, glacier or mountain, and forced to rely primarily on themselves for subsistence and security. But each settler was aware at the same time of being part of a larger community. Every June, after the collecting of the sea birds' eggs and after the sheep had been driven upland to their summer pastures, every farmer would gather up his family and some of his servants and slaves, and set off on a long jouncing pony-back journey to a spectacular, sunken, blackland plain 30 miles from present-day Reykjavik.

Here, beginning in 930, was held the meeting of the Althing, the people's general assembly. Following the oral and mnemonic tradition that gave rise to the sagas, an elected law speaker would each year recite from memory one third of the legal code of the land (page 128); the entire code took three years, and then a new man would start again.

If necessary, the laws were amended; suits were brought and adjudicated, marriages and other business deals were arranged and gossip exchanged, to an accompaniment of games and merrymaking and sometimes bloody fights over grievances old and new.

The Althing was Western Europe's first parliament. It was by no means democratic, for all real power was vested in 36 prominent landowners. Such a landowner, called a *godi* (priest), maintained a god's shrine on his property. The godi's function was to protect the interests of the neighboring, smaller farmers. In return, the 36 had a right to demand the help of their neighbors in their own disputes and feuds.

This arrangement was not ironclad and immutable, as it was in feudal

Grettir the Strong morosely grasps his sword and shield in this 17th Century Icelandic painting. Convicted of burning the home of an enemy with the man, his two sons and nine comrades trapped inside, Grettir was banished from civilization for 20 years. He insisted that the blaze was an accident, but his appeals for clemency were denied by the judges, one of whom declared, "If ever a man was doomed to misfortune, you are."

Europe. If a godi was weak or unreliable, his men could, and often did, transfer their allegiance to another. Nor was the average Icelandic farmer afraid of speaking up to his own or any other godi when he felt his family honor was at stake. There was more freedom of both thought and deed in Iceland than in virtually any other nation on earth at that time.

There was one grave weakness in the structure of the Icelandic commonwealth, however, one that would, after three centuries of health and prosperity, lead to anarchy and the loss of national independence. The Althing was both parliament and high court, but lacked an executive branch to enforce its decisions. Iceland had no army, no navy, no police, no taxes, no civil service of any kind. A blessed state, some would say. But it meant that if a man won a lawsuit at the Althing, he had no way to enforce the judgment or collect payment if the other party chose to be stubborn—no way, that is, unless he and his friends were strong enough to overawe the opponent and if necessary overcome him by brute force. This in turn could lead to attacks and counterattacks, battles, burnings, ambushes, killings and maimings, and endless blood feuds.

Feuds remained very much a part of daily life for these proud, touchy, battle-hardened men. And they could go on for generations—and leap far overseas, as in the tale of Grettir the Strong and his brother.

Grettir was a great warrior, and a conqueror of trolls and ghosts. But, alas, while exorcising a spirit, he fell under its spell, and thereafter was plagued by a murderous temper that soon got him outlawed. For 20 years, Grettir roamed the bleak interior until at last he returned to civilization—where his enemies quickly found and slew him.

His slayer, who soon became an outlaw himself, thereupon went off to Constantinople via Norway and for an adventure enlisted in the Varangian Guard. But he reckoned without Grettir's half brother, who lived in Norway. Swearing vengeance, the brother embarked for the same destination and he, too, enlisted in the Guard.

One day as they were lining up for parade, the killer boastfully pointed out the nick in his sword where it had broken Grettir's skull. The brother asked to inspect the weapon. When it was handed over, he brought it down into the killer's own skull. Redeeming family honor came before obedience to the regulations of any emperor, and the soldiers of the Guard loudly defended the deed of Grettir's brother.

There were only two ways of settling feuds, short of the complete extermination of one or the other party. One was a formal reconciliation, either privately or at the Althing, with payment of *wergild*, or "blood money," for each man slain. The other was for the Althing to declare one party guilty and condemn him to an existence outside the protection of the law for a period of years or for life—"unfeedable," as the laws put it, "unferriable, unfit for all help and shelter."

An outlaw might choose to disregard this decree, and many roamed the wilderness of Iceland's interior for years, living off blackmail and robbery. But such a man was fair game for anybody. He could be killed in any fashion at any time and no retribution money need be paid. Restless and desperate, hungering for refuge, some outlaws turned their eyes to the west, across the trackless ocean. And it was an outlaw named Eirik the Red who led the way.

The perilous voyage to Greenland the good

Of all the sea trails the Vikings blazed across the globe, none was so boldly chosen or so fraught with danger as the great arcing voyage that led from Iceland 800 miles across the North Atlantic to the southeast coast of Greenland.

The usual starting place for this voyage was Snaefellsnes, a craggy claw of land thrusting from the western side of Iceland. From that point the route was so perilous that the trip could be made only during the summer season. Even then the voyagers had to journey through the lower reaches of the arctic storm center, where gale-force winds and mighty seas devoured many a ship. Their course then cut directly across the path of the mammoth ice floes drifting south from the polar pack. At the end of the voyage a ship could still be smashed to kindling against the boulder-strewn shoals that guarded Greenland's eastern coast.

Despite all hazards, fleets of Viking ships set forth year after year in the 10th and 11th Centuries, packed with settlers and adventurers ready to risk their lives to start anew beneath Greenland's forbidding ice cliffs. For here and there, in protected fjords, Greenland offered gentle valleys carpeted with fine pastures and populated with game so plentiful and unaware that "a man," as a saga put it, "might bring down his quarry where he would, for all creatures there were placid and unafraid, knowing nothing of man."

The ship of choice for this voyage to what the Vikings called Greenland the Good was the beamy, deep-draft knarr, a durable merchantman that could transport about 30 persons with animals and household gear and frequently a cargo of timber as well—for although lush grasslands could be found, nothing larger than scrub birch grew in Greenland. The trip typically took about two weeks, although under the most favorable conditions it might be accomplished in four days. But many an unfortunate expedition was kept at sea by fog, adverse westerly winds and treacherous currents for a month or longer, and some—the Vikings did not dwell on how many—missed Greenland entirely and strayed off into the empty reaches of the Atlantic, never to be heard from again.

On a summer day at Snaefellsnes, Iceland, two oceangoing knarrs rest on the beach at low tide while their crews ready them to set out next morning for Greenland. On the vessel in the foreground, the mast is being hoisted into its step by means of a forestay and a crutch. Tools, weapons and household gear that will not be needed by the colonists until the ship reaches its destination have already been stowed under the fore and aft half decks, and now the men on shore are beginning to load hay for the animals and to trundle barrels of fresh water, dried fish and salted meat up the gangplank. The ship's boat is about to be stowed athwartships in the open hold. Last will come the waiting animals, which will ride amidships tethered to crossbeams.

With the wind gusting out of the northeast, the moment is right for the expedition to put to sea. On the vessel in the foreground the oars are being run in and stowed as the sail is hoisted. Women and children along the rail wave farewell to friends ashore as the helmsman swings the prow around to face the open ocean.

A second vessel pulls away from the shore under oar power while a third, whose keel still hangs on the bottom, is pushed clear by a gang of men. About five ships in all will attempt to make the journey to Greenland, traveling together in a convoy and following a route already well established during earlier migrations.

By nightfall the wind has shifted to the
west and the crew is busy rigging the
tacking spar, which will allow the ship
to make some progress against the weather.
In the stern a few settlers make a meal of
dried fish smeared with butter while others
rest huddled in their skin sleeping bags.
At the starboard rail the navigator takes a
sighting on the polestar, using a bearing
dial to determine his heading.

A sudden squall roaring out of the
southeast throws the ship's company into a
desperate struggle for survival. Loose
rigging snaps and slashes in the savage
winds. One man rushes amidships
with a bucket to clear the water flooding in
over the sides, while others attempt to
calm the terrified animals and protect the
children on the exposed deck. At the
stern a man heaves on the tiller to keep the
ship from broaching to in the huge waves.

Safely arrived on the west coast of Greenland, the weary, storm-tossed little band of settlers comes ashore at the first placid fjord to rest for a few days before heading north to the Viking settlement at Eiriksfjord. The cattle and sheep, having lived on fodder aboard ship, make straightaway for the beach grass along the shore.

The voyagers have had no hot food since leaving Iceland, and so, as a first order of business, two women knead pans of dough while, at left, another stirs a large caldron of porridge. In the background men wade out into the shallow water carrying a net to haul in some of the salmon teeming in the fjord.

The ships that were damaged in the storm have been beached and a crew of men works on the hulls, recaulking and refitting sprung and broken planks. Two of the ships will require new masts. The spare strakes and spars brought from Iceland are now crucial to complete the last leg of the journey up the coast.

To fuel the cooking fires, children have collected armloads of driftwood that has washed ashore from as far away as Russia. Although most of the settlers will spend the night in their sleeping bags on the ground, the leaders will sleep on beds and in the tents that are being assembled at right and center.

Chapter 6

Heroic discoverers of a new world

irik Thorvaldsson Raudi—Eirik the Red—was red of hair and red of beard, bloody of heart and bloody of hand. He was a murderously bad neighbor, a scoundrel on the grand scale, a heathen to the core, and to the very end he remained unregenerate. Yet he was a towering figure of a Viking. And others would follow him to the end of the world and live with him at the edge of human existence.

Cast out by his own society and driven by the forces of his own nature, Eirik thrust boldly toward the western horizon, where, on the perilous rim of Greenland's great permanent icecap, he founded a settlement that would survive for nearly five centuries as a monument to mortal endurance. Eirik's son Leif was less of an outcast. Yet within him stirred the same burning desire to reach westward beyond the wilderness of the ocean—and that hungering took him to the apogee of the Norse explorations: America, which Christopher Columbus was not to encounter for another half millennium.

Thus, step by step—from Norway to the Faroes to Iceland, Greenland and finally to America—the Vikings traversed the awesome North Atlantic, a perilous distance of more than 3,000 miles from the fjords of Norway, entrusting their lives to their own seamanship and their doughty little vessels. The sagas' accounts of the Norse adventure in America—or, as Leif named it, Vinland—are obscure, fragmentary and often frankly exaggerated. Precisely where the Vikings went, how long they stayed, what they did and why they left are pieces of a tantalizing puzzle. Equally baffling is the sudden and still unexplained disappearance of the Norsemen from the Greenland settlements to which they had clung so tenaciously for so long. Yet whatever the immediate (and perhaps inconsequential) details, the Norse withdrawal from Vinland and then from Greenland was part of the wormwood process of decay that brought an end to the great age of the Vikings.

Just as the Viking colonists faded into the mists of the sagas, so the Viking warriors, those "valiant, wrathful, purely pagan people" of the early Irish lament, gradually found themselves tamed and assimilated by the very peoples they had conquered in both east and west. Viking traders, too, saw themselves superseded by more powerful and sophisticated rivals. And though no one ever sailed more beautiful ships, the master builders of other lands devised craft that were so much larger and more useful that the Viking knarr and longship passed from the seas.

Eirik the Red was a sign and symbol of the great Viking age, and of its demise. He was born around 950 on a farm in southwest Norway. His violent nature found an early outlet. While Eirik was still in his late teens, he and his father, Thorvald, plunged—joyously, in all certainty—into one of the innumerable and interminable blood feuds that so fortified yet depleted Viking manhood. In the offhand words of a saga, there were "some killings." Eirik and Thorvald were outlawed and, like many outlaws before them, they followed their fate to Iceland.

They arrived late. By then, in the 960s, all of Iceland's good land had been taken, and what was left for recent outcasts was a rocky, hardscrabble tract on the cruel northwestern coast. Thorvald soon died, and Eirik

Looking more like a knight of the Round Table than a Viking pioneer, Eirik the Red, first colonizer of Greenland in 986, stands encased in full armor in this 17th Century Norwegian woodcut, one of the earliest representations of the Norwegian outlaw who found refuge and greatness by crossing the "Western Ocean."

was left to fend for himself—which he set about with a vengeance. He married Thjodhild, daughter of a prosperous family and, as it turned out, one of the few persons on earth whose willfulness matched Eirik's.

Eirik moved south and—probably with the help of his in-laws and perhaps by force—took and cleared land at Haukadal, an area of grass and birchwoods on an arm of the Breidafjord. But Eirik was never much for peaceful coexistence. Violence was always surging in his soul, and soon another feud resulted in the bloody deaths of two of his neighbors. Again Eirik was forced to flee. He dismantled his house, timber being too valuable in wood-scarce Iceland to leave behind, and moved to Oxney, on a Breidafjord promontory about 50 miles west of Haukadal.

Shortly after he arrived, in a rare moment of neighborliness, he loaned some of his house beams to a man named Thorgest, who wanted them briefly for his farmstead. But soon there came the inevitable day when Eirik, having decided where to settle permanently, was putting up his own house and demanded the return of his beams. Thorgest refused, thereby setting off yet another terrible feud. This one embroiled the entire countryside and brought violent death to two of Thorgest's sons. The vicious quarrel was finally resolved at the local assembly. Though his cause, for once, seemed entirely just, Eirik and his supporters were voted down by Thorgest's allies, and Eirik the Red was sentenced to three years' banishment from Iceland.

According to custom, he was given a few days' leave, and he used his time well. Thanks mostly to the affluence of his wife's family, he bought and provisioned a knarr, then set about collecting desperate men to accompany him on a desperate adventure. They were not hard to find. A few years before, Iceland had suffered a famine in which, according to a chronicler, "men ate ravens and foxes, and many loathsome things were eaten that should not be eaten, and some men had the old and helpless killed and thrown over the cliffs." The famine passed, but it left destitute many families, mostly the owners of marginal lands, whose strong sons and husbands were now eager to seek new fortune in a new land.

Eirik knew—more or less—where he wanted to go. More than 50 years before, sometime between 900 and 930, one Gunnbjorn Ulf-Krakason had been scooped up by a tremendous gale while he was sailing from Norway to Iceland, had missed his destination and had been storm-tossed far to the west. Eventually he sighted a cluster of tiny rock islands, and in the dim distance beyond them he spied the looming, shadowed form of a great land mass. But the place was not in the least inviting to Gunnbjorn. After naming the islets Gunnbjarnarsker, after himself, he put them in his wake the moment the wind turned fair, returning to his home in the same Breidafjord pocket of Iceland where, long after Gunnbjorn's death, Eirik the Red found his final Icelandic refuge.

Icelandic mariners had talked and speculated often about Gunnbjorn's islands, and at least one attempt had been made to explore this new corner of the earth. A man named Snaebjorn, seeking to escape retribution for a murder, had sailed in that direction with a number of companions in two boats. He found a little shelf of land at the edge of the monstrous icecap of Greenland, and there he built a dwelling. The arctic winter came howling down on the settlers, burying their house so deep

Half smothered with glaciers, Greenland (or Gronelanth, as it is labeled) is incorrectly connected to northern Europe through Lapland (called Pillappelanth) in this 15th Century map produced by cartographers at the Vatican. Completed at about the time Viking settlements in Greenland were dying out, the map bears Latin inscriptions at right noting the maximum hours of daylight at different latitudes, while at left an inscription identifies the Arctic Circle, marked with a thick gold line just north of Iceland.

in snow they had to dig a long tunnel upward to get out to the surface, so they could make their way down to their boats. They caught enough fish to keep from starving. But, cooped up in the fetid darkness, they allowed old rivalries and grievances to awake and, before they could get away in the spring, three men, including Snaebjorn himself, had been killed.

Eirik, of course, had heard the tale of Gunnbjorn's errant voyage, and of Snaebjorn's. The huge and mysterious mass sighted by Gunnbjorn could only have been the answer to Eirik's pagan prayers. In 982, at about 32 years of age, Eirik Thorvaldsson Raudi set forth.

The way was not particularly long, some 450 miles, and easy enough with good winds. Eirik sailed from under the Snaefellsnes, a glacial promontory that, like a giant index finger, points due west from Iceland's western coast. Moving steadily before the prevailing easterly breezes of early summer, Eirik tracked carefully along the 65th parallel, sighting the sun by day and Polaris by night. What Eirik and his crew beheld after four days or so of sailing was horrifying. Ranging before them, blinding in their brilliance beneath the sun, were cliffs that fell sheer from a monster icecap. As they approached, the Vikings could see the tips of enormous mountains peeking above the ice. The bravest of men might have been excused for turning back. But Eirik the Red coasted south. He may have stood out to sea and rounded Cape Farewell at the southeastern extremity of the new land. More likely, knowing that if grazing ground existed it would be found along the banks of the fjords, Eirik turned off, probing and feeling his way for mile after forbidding mile through a labyrinth of narrow, intersecting waterways until at last he made his exit on the western coast.

There he steered north, tracing along the twists and turns of the coastline, his sturdy knarr bobbing and weaving through the islands of an archipelago where the cliffs echoed the screams of millions of sea birds. Their cacophony was occasionally interrupted by a more ominous sound from starboard: the reports like cannon fire as huge icebergs broke from glaciers that overran the mainland's edge into the sea.

Yet, for all the glaciers, the permanent icecap itself did not reach to the western shore, which was instead fissured by countless fjords thrusting deep—in some cases more than 150 miles—into the interior. Their waters teemed with fish. Along their banks grew emerald grass; the ground was springy with moss and carpeted by a profusion of wild flowers—harebell, angelica, buttercups and pink wild thyme. It was at such a place, at the head of a broad and beautiful fjord that he naturally named after himself, Eiriksfjord, that Eirik the Red built his home.

Alone on the vast expanse of what was—although they could not know it—the world's largest island, Eirik and his followers soon found traces of previous human habitation. House ruins, fragments of boats, and stone implements bore witness to an earlier non-European culture. Indeed, man had been there as early as 2000 B.C.: a Stone Age reindeer-hunting people had lived there. They were succeeded around the beginning of the Christian era by people of the so-called Dorset culture, nomads who had neither kayaks nor dogs and whose survival depended on following the seals that provided them both food and clothing.

Eirik and his fellow Norsemen, then, were at least the third race to inhabit the huge island—and, as it turned out, the third to vanish from its face. But while they were there, the Vikings gave it a magnificent try. Eirik spent the remaining years of his exile from Iceland exploring the territory, making up such appealing place names as Eiriksfjord, Hvalsey Farm and Cape Farewell, and subdividing land among his followers. The forbidding place apparently enthralled him, and when, at the end of his banishment, he returned to Iceland to collect his wife, Thjodhild, and drum up more settlers, he gave his new country a name that carried monumental disregard for the truth. He called the island of the icecap Greenland—on the theory, as he acknowledged, that "men would be drawn to go there if the land had an attractive name."

Early in the summer of 986, Eirik the Red, thrice an outlaw and now the proud founder of a Viking colony, sailed from Iceland at the head of a fleet of 25 ships filled with men, women, children, and all their goods and chattels. The expedition was caught along the way by a storm—as so often happens, the saga fails to recount the harrowing details—that wrecked some of the vessels and forced others to turn back. But at last, 14 arrived safely, and nearly 400 persons went ashore to begin the colonization of Greenland.

These hardy pioneers went to work with a will. Unlike Iceland, Greenland had good stone for building, and the houses were thick walled with sod roofs. The homesteads were scattered along a 120-mile stretch of fjord-riven shoreline on the west coast. In time the settlers came to call this region the Eastern Settlement to distinguish it from the later—by 10 years—Western Settlement, some 300 miles to the north on a westward sweep of the land. The colonists soon adopted a constitution, established a national assembly and decreed a code of law, all based on Icelandic examples.

Although Eirik the Red may not have held official title, he was certainly the community's ruling patriarch. "His state was one of high distinction," acknowledges a saga, "and all recognized his authority." The Eastern Settlement eventually came to accommodate at least 190 farms; of them all, Eirik's Brattahlid, which was able to support 50 cows against an average 10 to 20 on other farms, was by far the finest. The Western Settlement eventually grew to encompass more than 90 farms, providing food and fiber for a total population that in the year 1100 A.D. reached about 3,000 people.

These were not warriors like Eirik but mostly solid yeoman farmers, crowded out of Iceland by implacable population pressures. They did so well that the word—perhaps colored by Eirik's far-reaching boasts— spread back to Norway. "It is reported," wrote a chronicler there, "that the pasturage is good and that there are large and fine farms in Greenland. The farmers raise sheep and cattle in large numbers and make butter and cheese in great quantities. The people subsist chiefly on these foods and on beef; they also eat the flesh of various kinds of game, such as caribou, whale, seal and bear."

But the farms alone could offer little more than a bare subsistence— and the Greenlanders had need of much else. They were wanting in iron for all purposes and especially for weapons. Although grain grew on a few sunny slopes, it was in piteously short supply. Beer and wine were required to satisfy the prodigious Viking thirst, as were European-style clothes and adornments to answer the craving for luxury items.

Most of all, the Greenlanders were extremely short of timber—absolutely essential if only for building and maintaining the ships that were their life line to the world. The local dwarf birch was useless for heavy duty, and reliance on driftwood, most of which followed the ocean currents on a long, looping route from Siberia, was chancy.

As it had been in Iceland, trade became a way of life. The farms could provide the fleece for Greenland woolen cloth, which counted as a valuable commodity in the trading towns of Scandinavia and elsewhere. In his only recorded lapse into moral turpitude, Eirik's son Leif, while journeying to Norway, once dallied awhile in the Hebrides, where he got a local highborn maiden with child. When she mentioned marriage, Leif paid her off with Greenland woolens and departed forthwith.

But the greatest natural trading treasures were to be found away from the farms in the wastelands of the far, far north, especially around Disco Bay on the 70th parallel. There, rough and hardy Norse hunters built rude stone shelters and set about reaping a precious harvest of wildlife.

With canoes and harpoons, they hunted the huge Greenland whale, which grew up to 70 feet long and could yield vast quantities of flesh and oil. There were even greater herds of ivory-tusked walrus and fat seal than in Iceland, and polar bears, only accidental in Iceland, were native to Greenland. The flocks of eider ducks were immense beyond belief and provided vast amounts of down for the quilts of Europe. And in the northern hunting grounds could be found the pure-white falcons so prized by medieval nobility.

The market for such goods was Europe, especially the Scandinavian trading towns, and commercial sailing routes were soon established. One was deemed worthy of detailed description in a saga: "From Hernar in Norway one must sail a direct course west to Hvarf in Greenland, in which case one sails north of Shetland so that one sights land in clear weather only, then south of the Faroes so that the sea looks halfway up the mountainsides, then south of Iceland so that one gets sight of birds and whales from there."

No matter how many times the trip was taken, it remained dangerous, and the sagas make frequent if passing mention of ships lost at sea. In addition to all the usual hazards, there lurked a phenomenon that one chronicler called "sea hedges," writing that it seemed "as if all the waves and tempests of the ocean have been collected into three heaps, out of which three billows have formed. These hedge in the entire sea, so that no opening can be seen anywhere; they are higher than lofty mountains and resemble steep, overhanging cliffs. In only a few cases have the men been known to escape who were upon the seas when such a thing occurred." Nothing recognized by science exactly fits this description. But the sea floor in the area is subject to earthquakes, which would produce tidal waves and unsettled sea conditions.

The mariners also risked daily death in their icy home waters. One of the most harrowing of the Greenland stories tells of Thorgils Orrabeinsfostri, who with his family (including an infant son) and some compan-

Emblazoned with a Viking ship, the seal of Bergen, Norway, reflects the importance of the city in the 13th Century as the principal port of trade with the Greenland colonies. The seal designer apparently chose esthetic composition over nautical accuracy by placing dragon heads at both ends of the ship; as a rule, dragon heads appeared on the bows only.

ions was shipwrecked in a storm that swept him onto the island's bleak east coast. Thorgils fashioned a crude boat from the wreckage of their craft. The castaways rowed hundreds of miles through icy channels and, when these became choked beyond passage, dragged their lifeboat across vast expanses of ice and snow. One by one the travelers dropped of cold and hunger, a grave-mantle of snow quickly covering their stiffening bodies. Thorgils' wife was among those who perished.

Finally, as his own end and that of his son drew near, Thorgils killed a polar bear with his sword, then clung grimly to its ears to prevent the great beast from slipping off the ice and sinking into the sea. With the meat of the bear in their bellies, Thorgils and his son survived.

Many another Greenland sailor in similar circumstance did not. One called Lika-Lodinn actually earned a living by collecting the dead bodies of shipwrecked seamen, boiling the flesh from the bones to make for lighter transportation, and carrying the skeletons back to the settlements for decent burial. For his efforts he understandably became known as Corpse-Lodinn.

Still, despite all hazard and hardship, the Greenland settlements not only continued to live and to grow, but even entered into a period of shaky prosperity. On his fjordside farm at Brattahlid, Eirik the Red had cause for satisfaction. Yet the late 990s, as he neared his 50th year, were for him a time of discontent. The place was becoming crowded; at least it appeared so to a man with a taste for open space. Moreover, civilization in the form of medieval Christianity was coming to Greenland—and Eirik's wife, Thjodhild, was one of the first and most passionate of the converts. To halt her nagging, Eirik finally permitted Thjodhild to build a chapel—on another fjord. As for being baptized himself, Eirik the Red drew a resolute line, much preferring to identify his own spirit with that of Thor and Odin. For his failure to take up the cross, Thjodhild barred him from her bed.

Small wonder, then, that Eirik Thorvaldsson Raudi longed for his lost youth and yearned for still more new lands to the west. In fact, such lands existed—and Eirik knew it.

Almost from the very time of Eirik's expedition to Greenland, an odd tale of exploration had been circulating among the Vikings. In late 985 a young Icelander named Bjarni Herjolfsson had made a trading voyage to Norway, wintered there and in the summer of 986 headed back to Iceland with a cargo of goods consigned to his father, Herjolf. By a matter of days, Bjarni arrived too late: Herjolf, evidently an impetuous sort, had sold his Iceland farm and accompanied Eirik the Red's little armada to Greenland. Dismayed but not daunted, Bjarni followed after his father, sailing due west for three days. Then a dense fog rolled in, followed by a north wind, and Bjarni's ship was tossed by storms for uncountable days in the gathering arctic winter.

When the storm finally abated, Bjarni sighted low, flat land covered by thick woods. This did not fit any description of Greenland given by Eirik to the Icelanders, so Bjarni sailed on, heading north. He came upon more land, similar to the first, and this time his crew, wishing to do a bit of exploring, set up a clamor to go ashore. No, replied the single-minded

High fashion for doughty settlers

Although life in Greenland was uncompromisingly plain and pioneer, the doughty colonists did strive to stay in touch with, and even emulate, the latest styles of medieval Europe. Rejecting the Eskimos' sealskin leggings and parkas, the Norsemen wove a durable cloth from the gray hairs of their sheep and fashioned all manner of woolen cloaks and gowns.

The settlers modeled their clothes on those worn by visiting merchants, and on what they saw during their own trading voyages to Iceland and Norway. They seem also to have written home for samples of the latest apparel. In 1308 the Bishop of Bergen sent to Bishop Thord at Gardar in Greenland a cloak, an overcoat and a pale-blue *kaprun*, or hood, lined with black skins, and with it a robe of the same color. Presumably these garments would be reproduced in homespun.

So modish were some Greenland colonists that they wore hoods with a long liripipe, or streamer, trailing down behind. While the liripipe was originally used to store valuables or to secure the hood at the neck, dandies wore hoods with streamers that touched the ground.

With a high peak and decorative streamer, this woolen Greenland hood aped 14th Century European styles.

Bjarni. He was searching for Greenland, which had glaciers, and here there were no glaciers. On again sailed Bjarni, carried by a southwest wind for three days until he came abreast of bare, black cliffs rising like vertical slabs from the sea. There were plenty of glaciers here, stupendous ones, looming up in the distance and disgorging into the sea through breaks in the cliffs.

Bjarni did not even lower his sails. "This land looks good for nothing," he pronounced, and now he steered to the east, where, after four more days, he finally came upon a land that perfectly matched the description of Greenland he had been carrying around in his head.

He rounded a cape. There was his father's ship and there was his father. Bjarni Herjolfsson delivered his cargo and, his filial duty done, settled down to a quietly productive life on Greenland. He never knew that he had discovered America.

Now, at the turn of the millennium, Eirik the Red had been hearing the story of Bjarni's voyage for nearly 15 years. To a man of his disposition, fretted by domestic annoyances, the call of the mysterious land to the west must have sounded as strongly as ever. He was, however, an old man by Viking standards, and he might not be able to stand the trip. But his son Leif could, and did.

Leif was a golden Viking. One saga describes him as "a big, strapping fellow, handsome to look at, thoughtful and temperate in all things." He was a splendid seaman, his reputation already firmly established as the first Viking shipmaster to make direct voyages with trade goods between Greenland, Scotland and Norway and back again. These were bold ventures, accomplished by sailing along the 60th parallel for 1,800 miles without sight of land. But his courage was tempered by prudence, and he was not a sort to fare blindly into the unknown. Instead, before questing Bjarni's new lands, he sought Bjarni's advice, soliciting information about routes and landmarks, winds and currents, rocks and shoals. Only then, in the summer of 1001, after purchasing Bjarni's ship and collecting a crew of 35, was Leif ready. Eirik had meant to go along, and even to assume nominal command. But on the way to the shore where the ship awaited, his horse stumbled and threw Eirik, and the old fellow broke his leg. "I am not meant to discover more countries than this one we are now in," he said to his son. "This is as far as we go together."

Because he had been wind-blown and lost during the first part of his 986 voyage, Bjarni Herjolfsson had been able to provide Leif with specific sailing instructions only about the last leg. Leif therefore followed Bjarni's route in reverse, first sailing due west until he came upon the dismal, glacier-topped rock pile that Bjarni had deemed useless to anyone. Leif anchored briefly, going ashore for an inspection and concluding that Bjarni had been quite correct. After naming the place Helluland—Flatland—he got under way as swiftly as possible and sailed south, leaving behind him what was surely Baffin Island, most easterly of the islands of the Canadian arctic archipelago, and separated from Labrador by 250 miles of the Hudson Strait.

Leif next put his ship's boat ashore at the place where Bjarni had refused to stop, despite the persistence of his crew. "This country," relates a saga, "was level and wooded, with broad white beaches wherever they went and a gently sloping shoreline." The Norsemen, accustomed both in Scandinavia and in the western settlements to cramped and rocky shores, called these beaches Wonder Strands. Behind the beaches was another marvel: vast stands of gigantic trees tall and sturdy enough to make a timber-poor Greenlander's heart sing. The physical description given in the sagas corresponds to a 30-mile stretch of fine beaches, backed by spruce woodlands, along the Labrador coast between lat. 53° 45' N. and 54° 09' N. in the vicinity of Cape Porcupine. Leif named it Markland, or Land of Forests.

Enticing though Markland must have been, Leif was determined to explore farther. Relates a saga: "After sailing two *doegr*, they sighted another shore and landed on an island to the north of the mainland." In this case, a *doegr*, a measure of both time and distance, probably meant a two-day journey of about 165 miles. The island on which they landed was doubtless Belle Isle, about 15 miles north of Newfoundland and northeast of the Gulf of St. Lawrence. There Leif and his men found the grass heavy with dew, which they collected and drank—"and thought they had never known anything so sweet as that was."

"Then," continues the saga, "they returned to the ship and sailed through the channel between the island and a cape jutting out to the north of the mainland"—almost certainly Cape Bauld, Newfoundland. "They steered a westerly course past the cape and found great shallows at ebb tide, so that their ship was beached some distance from the sea." When the tide rose, the adventurers towed their knarr off the sandbar, and they "took their leather sleeping bags ashore and built themselves shelters. Later they decided to stay there during the winter and set up large houses. There was no lack of salmon either in the river or in the lake, and these salmon were bigger than any others the men had ever seen. Nature was so generous here that it seemed to them that cattle would need no winter fodder but could graze outdoors. There was no frost in winter, and the grass hardly withered. The days and nights were more nearly equal than in Greenland or Iceland. On the shortest day of winter the sun remained up between breakfast time and late afternoon."

The saga was almost surely exaggerating the benignity of the Newfoundland climate. Nevertheless, it may well have seemed like Elysium compared to what the men had experienced on Greenland in the dark months. In fact, all through the winter, Leif sent out parties of exploration to investigate the surrounding countryside. One evening the man Leif called his "foster father" failed to return from a scouting expedition. He was a German crony of Eirik the Red's named Tyrkir, and his role, as was customary among well-positioned Vikings, was to serve Leif as a sort of stand-in father on the voyage, seeking to guard him from harm, offering him counsel and tutoring him in various ways. Naturally, Leif mounted an anxious search, and finally Tyrkir was found in a condition of great excitement. "I have some real news for you," he cried. "I have found grapevines and grapes!"

"Is this possible, Foster Father?" asked Leif.

"Certainly," replied Tyrkir, "for I was born where there is no lack of either vines or grapes."

Unearthed in a churchyard in western Greenland and made of Labrador quartzite—a kind of flint not found in Greenland—this arrowhead suggests that the Vikings did indeed make contact with North American Indians somewhere along the coast of Canada. The arrowhead dates back to around 1000, precisely the time when the Viking seafarers claimed to have made landfalls in the New World beyond Greenland.

So saying, he led Leif to the place where he had made his astonishing find—and there they were, vines laden with fruit. "And," the saga relates, "it is said that they loaded up the afterboat with grapes, and the ship itself with a cargo of timber. When spring came, they made the ship ready and sailed away. Leif gave this country a name to suit its products. He called it Vinland"—Wineland.

Tyrkir's grapes would confound future generations. Were it not for them, there would likely be little dispute about the location of Leif's Vinland as being at L'Anse aux Meadows in the Sacred Bay area at the northern tip of Newfoundland. Geographically and in physical details, the place fits the sagas: Epaves Bay, an inlet of Sacred Bay, is shallow, with rocks that would hang up a Viking knarr at low tide; the natural meadow is among the largest in northern Newfoundland. Nearby, curving to the sea, is Black Duck Brook, up which salmon run to spawn in the spring. South of the meadow stands an extensive spruce forest. Finally, and seeming to clench the case, the remains of what were almost certainly Norse buildings have been found at L'Anse aux Meadows and nowhere else in America.

But how to explain the grapes? In plain fact, grapes could not have grown in the vicinity of L'Anse aux Meadows, or anywhere else so far north. Because of this discrepancy, frequent and serious efforts have been made to place Vinland along the east coast of America from Nova Scotia as far south as Florida. Other attempts, often ingenious and occasionally persuasive, have sought a semantic solution. Thus, for example, if a scribe had been confused between the Norse words *vín* (long i), for "wine," and *vin* (short i), for "pasture," that might account for the conflict—were it not that the sagas specifically mention clusters of grapes (*vínber*) from which wine could be made.

It is possible that the sagas used the word grape in only the loosest of senses—to mean a roundish fruit. In that case Tyrkir's "grapes" may have been squashberries, gooseberries, cranberries or currants, all of which could be made into wine and all of which grew in the north. There is no Old Norse name for these fruits. But *vínber* translates literally as "wineberry," and thus it could have been applied to a number of plants in addition to grapes.

Strangely, throughout decades of debate, the simplest explanation of the grapes has been largely ignored. Leif was, after all, the son of Eirik the Red—the man who had attracted settlers to one of the bleakest places on earth by touting it as a lush Greenland. With that remarkably successful example in mind, Leif could hardly have been above gilding his American discovery by calling it Vinland and saying that he returned with a cargo of grapes.

That he intended eventually to establish a permanent settlement in Vinland is beyond doubt. But Leif himself would not be one of the settlers: shortly after his return to Greenland, Eirik the Red died, and Leif assumed the duties and responsibilities of running the farm at Brattahlid. His seafaring days were done. However, his brother Thorvald, arguing that more exploration was needed before any attempt at colonization, outfitted his own ship and took on a crew. He followed Leif's route and wintered at Leif's temporary huts in Vinland, living mostly on fish.

In spring and summer he scouted up and down the coast in the ship's tender, finding little of note and spending a second winter in the old camp. Next summer he probed the coastline again, this time in the ship itself. A storm drove it ashore on a promontory—it could have been any one of several between Cape Bauld and Cape Porcupine—breaking the keel. Thorvald apparently effected repairs with local timber and set the broken keel erect in the sand to serve as a landmark.

Despite this mishap, the expedition had so far been rather well managed. But now, at another cape, came one of those senseless outbursts of savagery that so flawed the Viking character. After spotting three skin boats, overturned on the beach with three men sleeping beneath each, the Norsemen killed all but one, who escaped. In this murderous fashion the Vikings introduced themselves to the Skraelings—an obscure term that may have meant "wretches" or "weaklings" or "screechers" or "pygmies" or one of several other epithets of low regard. They may have been either Eskimos or Algonquin Indians—both lived in the area. Whoever they were, they soon appeared in raging, overwhelming force at the scene of the killings.

Fleeing to their ship, the Norsemen took their customary defensive position behind a gunwale hung with shields. The Skraelings loosed a hail of arrows, a number of which penetrated the barricade and one of which struck Thorvald in an armpit. It is not recorded whether the arrow was dipped in poison or some other septic substance. In any case, the wound festered and proved mortal. The survivors buried their slain leader between two crosses at the site of the keel-landmark, wintered again at Leif's stopping place and finally returned to Greenland, as a saga laconically put it, with "plenty of news to tell Leif."

Another of Eirik's sons, a lad named Thorstein, set out to retrieve his brother's body. But he managed only to get himself caught in a series of storms that flung him hither and yon—at one point east past Iceland almost as far as Ireland—for an entire summer.

At last, in 1009, a determined attempt was made to establish a settlement in Vinland. Curiously, it was led not by a Greenlander but by an Icelander: Thorfinn Karlsefni—Thorfinn the Valiant, as he came to be known. He was a young merchant who, in plying his trade between Norway and Greenland, got to know Eirik's sons and married Gudrid, the comely widow of Thorstein, Leif's brother who had since died of a fever. Through them he became fascinated with Vinland. Thorfinn put together a full-fledged expedition, with three ships carrying 250 persons, including some wives and, relates a saga, "all kind of livestock, for it was their intention to colonize the country if they could."

Taking the route established by Leif, Thorfinn and his followers found Vinland and took residence in—and doubtless built additions to—Leif's houses, where Gudrid gave birth to a son, Snorri, the first European child born in America.

After a cruel winter, during which they were forced to fight and kill ravenous forest bears, the settlers sailed southward until they came to a sheltered place with good pasturage that they named Hóp, an Old Norse word for a small, landlocked bay. There they met and entered into trade with another tribe of Skraelings, filthy creatures with, says a saga, "ugly

Wearing massive crowns and regal robes, four kings of the Norwegian dynasty that came to rule Greenland appear stern and mighty in this 16th Century woodcut. Founder of the dynasty in 1184, Sverrir Sigurdsson (top left) revitalized lagging Norwegian foreign trade, and his grandson Hakon (top right) formally annexed Greenland in 1261. Hakon's son Magnus (bottom left) continued to support trade with Greenland, but his weak son Eirik helped bring on the decline in commerce that eventually doomed the colonists.

hair on their heads, big eyes and broad cheeks." To their great gratification, the Vikings discovered that these Skraelings were willing to trade valuable furs for cow's milk or a span of red cloth to wrap around their heads. As if that were not enough, the Vikings, says a saga, delightedly compounded the swindle: "When the cloth began to run short, they cut it up so that it was no broader than a fingerbreadth, but the Skraelings gave just as much, or more."

The Skraelings were not so simple as they seemed. They perceived that the Vikings' metal swords were far superior to their own stone weapons, and they were vastly annoyed when Thorfinn forbade his men to trade away any swords. Inevitably, a Skraeling tried to steal a sword; just as surely, he was killed. A screaming mob of Skraelings attacked in overwhelming force, and with a weird weapon of primitive psychological warfare. It was described in a saga as "a pole with a huge knob on the end, black in color and about the size of a sheep's belly, which flew over the heads of the men and made a frightening noise when it fell." This strange object panicked the Vikings; the knob was probably nothing more than a blown-up moose bladder. Thorfinn and his men in short order were driven to a last stand with their backs against a cliff. There they would certainly have been massacred had it not been for Freydis, a bastard daughter of Eirik's and as bloodthirsty a character as can be found in the sagas. She ripped open her bodice, pulled out a breast and slapped it with the flat of a sword, as if infusing it with some magical power. The primitive Skraelings, astounded by this display and possibly thinking her some sort of female warrior-god, turned and fled in terror.

Although the would-be settlers lingered in America for two more years, they lost heart in the face of the Skraelings' continuing harassment and finally departed. "It now seemed plain," explains a saga, "that though the quality of the land was admirable, there would always be fear and strife dogging them there on account of those who already inhabited the land." Thorfinn's was the last significant Norse effort to settle America, although as late as 1341 there was a report of a Greenland ship making a trip to Labrador, probably on a timber-cutting mission.

By then, Greenland itself was in the throes of terrible troubles. After 1200 the entire North Atlantic area entered into the so-called Little Ice Age, when glaciers began growing bigger and sea temperatures dropped drastically. For the Greenland settlements the result was disastrous: there was a vast increase in the ice drifting south with the East Greenland Current and, as a result, the island's sea approaches, always difficult, were rendered perilous in the extreme. In the middle of the 13th Century a chronicler reported: "As soon as one has passed over the deepest part of the ocean, he will encounter such masses of ice in the sea that I know no equal of it anywhere else in all the earth. Sometimes these ice fields are about four or five ells thick"—that is, eight feet—"and extend so far out from the land that it may mean a journey of four days or more to travel across them. There is more ice to the northeast and north of the land than to the south, southwest and west. It has frequently happened that men have sought to make the land too soon and, as a result, have been caught in the ice floes. Some of those who have been caught have perished."

Tragic tale of clashing cultures

The Greenlanders' trading economy, precarious at best, could withstand little such disruption, and in 1261 the desperate islanders sought succor, surrendering their precious independence to Norway in return for various trade concessions—which the Norwegian kings, whether by neglect or malice, never lived up to. A year later, Iceland, under the same pressures of declining trade and increasingly bitter cold, also sought help from the Crown of Norway—with much the same result, though the Icelanders in the end survived while the Greenlanders did not.

Besides ice, the cold brought a new menace to Greenland in the person of Skraelings—this time Eskimos of the Thule culture who in an epochal migration had moved from Alaska across northern Canada to Ellsmere Island and thence, in their pursuit of the cold-loving seal, to the northernmost reaches of Greenland.

Relations between the two peoples soon turned violent. Few records of the fighting survive, but there is little doubt that it was bloody—and uneven. The Eskimos were in their natural element, all but oblivious to the cold and wise to every way of the north. The Viking hunters, no matter how skilled with weapons, were alien to this brutal land. They suffered from the cold, from lack of proper food at times, from Eskimo ambushes (pages 154-158). The Norsemen slowly withdrew before the Eskimo advance, until they finally abandoned the Western Settlement and moved to the Eastern Settlement, where they prepared for a last stand. The sagas do not say whether the Western Settlement was abandoned in haste under attack. But it may have been; many years later a Norwegian investigator sent out to examine conditions in Greenland reported that the Eskimos in control of the settlement had "many horses, goats, cattle and sheep."

For some reason, perhaps because the seal herds led the way, the Eskimos' advance took them to the southeast, all the way to Cape Farewell, bypassing the Eastern Settlement, which clung grimly to life until about 1500—when complete silence fell upon the community founded by Eirik the Red. Whether the Norsemen were wiped out by returning Eskimos, by pirates then roaming the North Atlantic or by some natural disaster is unknown. History records only that in 1586 the English explorer John Davis, seeking the Northwest Passage, put into a Greenland fjord along whose banks a Viking settlement had once burst with energy and throbbed with hope. He may have found some ruins, but no living person—"nor anything, save only gripes, ravens and small birds, such as larks and linnets."

The last traces of life in the Eastern Settlement have been found on a farm located on the next fjord over from Eirik's Brattahlid. There was a barrel with the bones of a hundred mice that had climbed in when it still contained milk and had starved to death when there was no more. Nearby in the farmyard were the bones of a Norseman. He may have been the last descendant of Eirik the Red. Since there was no one left to bury him, his bones remained where he lay down to die.

The disappearance of the Greenland settlements was only part of a long and sweeping evolution that finally closed out the age of the Vikings. At least in part, the Vikings fell victim to their own extraordinary success.

Among the tragedies that befell the Greenland settlers was a series of violent encounters with nomadic Eskimos pressing inexorably down from the north in pursuit of seals. Norse tradition has not dealt with this clash of cultures, except to record one incident that occurred in the 14th Century and that ended in disaster for the Greenland Norsemen. But tales of the confrontation were preserved in the rich oral history of the Eskimos, and after many centuries they were at last committed to writing.

The scribe was an Eskimo hunter by the name of Aron who was confined to bed with tuberculosis during the 1860s. He occupied himself by illustrating and then recording in writing the legend of the early encounters between the Eskimos and the Viking settlers. His watercolors, some of which are reproduced at right and on the following pages, are among the treasures of Greenland folk art.

The tale begins with Eskimo hunters paddling along in their umiak (top right) at the moment they spied a strange new house in one of Greenland's many fjords. As the Eskimos approached, a group of k'avdlunaks—foreigners—emerged from the dwelling. The k'avdlunaks were Norsemen, continued Aron. "The Greenlanders were afraid of these Norsemen, though they showed themselves friendly."

At first a wary cordiality existed between the two peoples. But then, said Aron, an evil Greenlander girl, Navaranak, set out to make trouble. She told the Norsemen: "The Greenlanders are beginning to be very angry with you!" To her countrymen she whispered, "The k'avdlunaks are preparing to do away with you!"

One day when the Eskimo men were all out hunting, the Norsemen, believing her lies, fell murderously upon the Eskimo women and children. Two women attempted to flee. One made good her escape; the other one the Norsemen "hewed at with axes and killed not only the mother but the child."

The Eskimo hunters were wild with grief and rage. With a magician's aid, said Aron, one hunter "built an umiak that would enable him to revenge himself on the Norsemen." This umiak was built to look "like a piece of dirty ice," and within this disguised vessel the Eskimos could drift to shore undetected.

Surprise was complete. The Greenlanders

waited until the Norsemen were in the house, then went ashore to burn it down. "Not until the entrance was in flames did the Norsemen notice anything wrong," recounted Aron. Those who fled came under a hail of Eskimo arrows.

Ungortok, chieftain of the Norsemen, leaped from a window, hugging his small son. The unarmed Ungortok could escape only by dropping his child into a nearby lake and leaving him to drown. "Bitterness added wings to his flight," wrote Aron, and Ungortok outran his Eskimo pursuers. Only one other Norseman escaped, a man who made it to a ship and outsailed the Greenlanders' umiaks.

In conclusion Aron related: "The Greenlanders turned their last anger against the disturber of the peace, Navaranak, dragging her along the ground until death. She had destroyed the friendship of Greenlanders and Norsemen. From that day there were no longer any Norsemen in any of the fjords."

Eskimo hunters stumble upon a Norse settlement in Greenland. As related by the Eskimo scribe and illustrator Aron, they saw the house "but as yet there were no people to be seen."

All was peaceful at the first meeting between Eskimos and Norsemen. In fact, wrote Aron, "The arrival of the umiak amused the Norsemen greatly."

The Norsemen, misled by an Eskimo girl, attack the camp and kill the Greenlander women, the only ones at home.

One woman escaped the carnage, and she "returned to the tents," recorded Aron, "where she found all the others lying slain."

Even the wary Norsemen are fooled by the icelike camouflage of the umiak of the vengeance-seeking hunters. According to Aron, one Norseman saw through the ruse and shouted, "Here come the Eskimos!" But another man scoffed, "That is no boat, it is merely some floes!"

Driven by their wrath, the Eskimos set fire to the Norsemen's house. In Aron's account, "Most of those who tried to force their way out perished in the flames, while the Greenlanders killed with arrows the few who were lucky enough to slip through the conflagration."

In order to escape, Ungortok sacrifices his son. "He kissed his little son repeatedly," wrote Aron, "and threw him into the lake."

A second Norseman flees by ship, crying to the hills, "Send me now your strong morning breeze" —which did happen.

In the great explosion of their energy, they had crossed the seas to conquer. In the enjoyment of their gains, they had settled down to rule. And in their rule, they erected defensive barriers against further expansion from the Norse homelands.

In the East the Viking princes and grand dukes had mingled and intermarried so thoroughly with their Slavic subjects that they turned Slav themselves. When Svyatoslav of Kiev—among the first of the Viking dynasty to bear a non-Scandinavian name—conquered Bulgar on the Volga in about 970, he all but severed the major trade routes through Russia to the Norselands, and turned his attention east to Byzantium, whose Orthodox Christian faith his people would soon wholeheartedly adopt. In the West another Viking descendant, William of Normandy, organized and led the conquest of England in 1066. The sons and grandsons of the Vikings were assimilated into that society. Viking blood flowed in the veins of King Harold of England; many of his warriors remembered their Viking ways, despite conversion to Christianity, and stood shoulder to shoulder, swinging their great battle-axes—until they were finally overwhelmed by the Norman host (*pages 162-169*).

In Norway the boil of Viking blood seemed to cool with succeeding generations. Harald Hardradi, who had died a Viking hero's death in England fighting the English in 1066 shortly before the Norman invasion, was followed by his son Olaf, who was contemptuously called the Quiet because, unlike all his ancestors, he fought no wars. His own son and successor, Magnus, known as Bareleg because he liked to wear Celtic kilts, entertained dreams of glory and mounted a number of expeditions to the Hebrides and to Ireland. But he was a failure as a warrior and was cut down in battle with the Irish before he accomplished much of anything. And Magnus' sons, Sigurd and Eystein, who divided up his kingdom in Norway, summed up in their characters and careers all the difference between the old sanguinary Viking days and the new, less violent, more Europeanized Scandinavia that was coming to birth.

King Sigurd was a throwback. Off at 17 on a crusade to the Holy Land in 1106, he performed deeds of high valor in Spain and in Syria, rode in state through Jerusalem and Constantinople, and after three years came back to Norway bearing a fragment of the True Cross. There was, of course, a feast, featuring a traditional boasting match in which each man tried to outvie his neighbor in accounts of his fearsome exploits.

"The expedition I made out of the country was a princely expedition," said Sigurd tauntingly to his brother, Eystein, "while you in the meantime sat at home like your father's daughter. I was in many a battle in the Saracens' land and gained the victory in all, and you must have heard of the many valuable articles I acquired, the like of which were never seen before in this country. I went to Palestine, but I did not see you there, Brother. I went all the way to Jordan, where our Lord was baptized, and swam across the river. But I did not see you there either."

Eystein answered with a negation of the whole Viking heritage. "I have heard that you had several battles abroad," he said, "but what I was doing in the meantime here at home was more useful for the country. In the north at Vaage I built fish houses so that all the poor people could get a living and support themselves. The road from Drontheim goes over the

Dovrefjelds, and many people had to sleep out-of-doors, and made a very severe journey, but I built hospices, and all travelers know that Eystein has been king in Norway. Out in Agdaness was a barren waste, and no harbor, and many a ship was lost there, and now there is a good harbor and ship station, and a church also built there. I raised beacons. I built a royal hall and the church of the apostles. I settled the laws, Brother, so that every man can obtain justice from his fellow man, and according as these are observed, the country will be better governed. Now although all this that I reckoned up be but small doings, yet I am not sure if the people of the country have been better served by it than by your killing for the devil in the land of the Saracens and sending them to hell.''

The future was to lie with Eystein, while Sigurd's crusade was but the last spark of a fading fire. Even if the will had been there, the physical wherewithal for the Viking life was disappearing. What had made the Viking adventure possible in the first place was control of the seas; now other seafarers with bigger ships were supplanting the Norsemen.

Europe—partly owing to the whiplash of Viking activity—had roused from the torpor of the Dark Ages and was in a state of vigorous economic expansion, with commerce flowing along its waterways under the protection of strong and relatively stable states. There was less need for the light Viking craft that could dart in and out of beaches with a load of luxury goods. These goods, along with bulkier products—grain, coal,

While gravediggers hastily carve out fresh graves, a grim parade of pallbearers arrives at a cemetery with the coffins of plague victims, in an illumination from a French manuscript of the 14th Century. Such scenes were common in 1349, when the Black Death ravaged Europe and Scandinavia. Norway lost nearly one third of its population; the loss crippled commerce and virtually halted the meager trade with the Greenland settlers.

cloth—could be carried more efficiently in the commodious cogs of the north German merchants grouped in the league known as the Hansa. The cogs were single-masted, square-rigged vessels, squat, unlovely and slow, but they could carry hundreds of tons of cargo, which made up for all their shortcomings.

The Hanseatic merchants who built and operated great fleets of such cogs were tough and ruthless competitors, far better organized than the individualistic Vikings. The league was first formed in 1158 and became in 1240 an association of north German cities—Lübeck, Hamburg, Bremen, Rostock, Kiel and Danzig—that banded together for mutual protection and the promotion of trade. By the 13th Century a dozen or so Baltic ports were in the league, and even cities in the German Rhineland, notably Cologne, joined to give the Hansa an effective monopoly on north European trade.

When the Scandinavian kings needed cash to pay for their elaborate courts and castles, they were forced to borrow it in exchange for trading privileges that eventually became monopolies in Scandinavia also. By the end of the 13th Century, the Hansa had a strangle hold on all the commerce of the North.

A Norwegian nobleman, dreaming that the world had not changed since the days of his Viking ancestors, made some raids on German shipping. Reprisal came quickly and devastatingly, in the form of a blockade of all Norwegian ports. The King of Norway was compelled to capitulate, pay a huge fine and make vast new concessions to the Hansa, culminating in the league's ownership of his biggest port at Bergen.

The passing of the Viking days and ways was galling enough to the Norwegians, the Danes, the Swedes. For the Icelanders it was a calamity.

As long as Norse ships passed regularly over the northern ocean, transporting goods and fighting men and tales of valor, Iceland could be an organic part of the vigorous Viking life. Without trees the Icelanders could not build their own ships; with a declining commerce they could not buy new ones abroad. As the years went by and the climate grew colder, and the ice floes pressed farther south, the Icelanders found themselves relegated more and more to a peripheral position, neglected and half forgotten in a distant and desolate outpost. The population declined dramatically, and it seemed entirely possible that Iceland would disappear from the map of the inhabited world. Somehow the Icelanders held on, though they lost their cherished independence.

It was during this 13th Century period of darkness that Snorri Sturluson, one of Iceland's greatest poets, wrote the saga of his great ancestor, Egil Skallagrimsson. As he wrote, he knew that his own days were numbered; Snorri was a colossal brawler as well as a writer, and he had made many enemies who yearned for his life. Quoting from Egil's ode on the death of his son, Snorri protests against Hel, the goddess of death, in verse that stands as an epitaph to the whole doomed age of the Vikings:

The end is all;/Even now
High on the headland/Hel stands and waits.
Life fades, I must fall/And face my own end,
Not in misery and mourning/But with a man's heart.

A bloody contest for supremacy among Viking heirs

The Norman conquest of England in 1066 was typical of the internecine wars fought by Viking against Viking toward the end of their era—and by the descendants of Vikings in violent rivalry for control of lands they had adopted. The struggle for the throne of England pitted Saxon King Harold Godwinson, a descendant of Danish and Swedish kings, against Duke William of Normandy, who traced his lineage to the great Norwegian chieftain Rollo.

The issue was settled by awful carnage on Senlac Hill near Hastings on October 14, 1066. But once he became master of England, William brutally set about blocking further Scandinavian influence in England. He introduced medieval French systems of government, land ownership, economics and thought. Thus he helped bring about the end of Europe's Viking age, replacing it with a new feudal era that fixed the map of Europe for the next 400 years.

The heroic figures and grisly deeds climaxing that blood-soaked autumn day on the rolling green south coast of England are preserved by an epic saga in linen, the only complete piece of narrative needlework to survive the Middle Ages—the Bayeux Tapestry. More than 230 feet long and 20 inches wide, the embroidery, segments of which are shown at right and on the following pages, was worked in eight colors of wool on a bleached linen field. It was executed soon after the invasion, presumably by William the Conqueror's wife, Matilda, and her ladies in waiting, to serve as a commemorative wall hanging for the Cathedral of Bayeux in Normandy. Incredibly, the embroidery survived two 12th Century fires and the pillaging of subsequent wars.

As tapestry and plot unfold, Danish King Knut, who ruled England, has died and his two inept sons have split the Danish-Saxon confederation. Saxon nobles crown one of their own, Edward the Confessor, King of England. The weak-willed Edward promises his throne to both Harold Godwinson of Wessex and Duke William of Normandy, and when Edward dies in January 1066, Harold claims the throne. William is outraged, insisting Harold had sworn allegiance to him, and begins planning the invasion.

Circumstances now conspire against Harold. Faced by a Norwegian invasion in the north, Harold leaves the south unguarded. After destroying the Norwegians, he learns that William has landed unopposed near Hastings. Harold hurries his weary forces south to meet the enemy host—and there, as the tapestry records, the historic battle unfolds.

Building the Norman fleet, woodsmen beside a stone watchtower fell trees while Norman sawyers—themselves probably descendants of Viking invaders in France—use adzes to shape planking in traditional Scandinavian boatbuilding methods. At right, dragon-prowed longships, following Viking designs, take shape as shipwrights trim gunwales and cut oar holes.

Acclaimed by Saxon nobles, Harold assumes England's throne in the new Westminster Abbey, blessed by Archbishop Stigand (right). The Latin reads, "Here sits Harold, King of the English."

Denouncing Harold as a treacherous usurper, Duke William (seated left) plots revenge with the Bishop of Bayeux (seated right) and orders his shipwrights to construct a huge invasion fleet.

Under Latin words relating "The ships are dragged to the water," Norman serfs strain with ropes and pulleys to launch the great fleet totaling 700 craft. But contrary winds blowing out of the north delayed the sailing of William's armada until autumn. Along its top and bottom borders the tapestry is embellished with a menagerie of silhouetted creatures both real and fabulous.

Tunics of chain mail, each so heavy it requires two serfs to carry, are taken to the ships along with provisions for the coming campaign. "These men," says the Latin, "are carrying arms to the ships and here they are dragging a cart laden with wine and arms"—helmets and lances among them. A strict disciplinarian, William slaked the army's thirst but forbade drunkenness.

When a strong east wind at last comes up, the invaders set sail at night, their vessels loaded with weapons and horses. "Their numberless masts clustered together looked like trees in a forest," wrote William of Poitiers, chaplain to Duke William. The Duke's single-masted ship is in the center of the fleet, identified by a wealth of shields and the square lantern at the masthead.

ADNAVES:ETHIC +HIC:VVILLELM:DVX INMAGN:O:

RAHVNT:CARRVM

VMVINO:ETARMIS:

Leading his nobles to the armada under the Latin "Here is William," the Duke rides a high-stepping charger presented to him by the King of Aragon (extreme right). Over eight months he had assembled an army of 11,000 warriors, including Swedish and Danish Vikings and German knights. But the heart of the army was 3,600 Norman horsemen, equipped with kite-shaped shields.

ÆÆÆ:·: HIC EXEVNT

They "crossed the sea and came to Pevensey," the Latin says of their arrival at dawn —a ghostly host of dragon ships. With King Harold still in the north heading off a Norwegian attack, the advantage of surprise was with the Normans. England's Channel coast was undefended, and the Normans began furling their square-rigged sails and poling their ships ashore.

DENAVIBVS:- ET hIC:MILITES: FESTINA VERV N

Beaching their ships and landing horses, the Normans with lances poised gallop across the countryside and up the coast to the port of Hastings. "Here the soldiers have hastened to Hastings to seize food," recounts the Latin. The port served a dual purpose for William—as both campaign headquarters and a handy place from which to escape across the Channel if he was defeated.

ASTELLVM:AT hESTENGA CEASTRA HIC:NVNTIATVM EST: WILLELM DEHAROLD:

Preparing for a siege at Hastings if need be, one of William's nobles, standing at far left, supervises the building of a castle and palisade to defend their position, with serfs and soldiers as laborers. Then, according to the Latin, William hears from a scout that Harold is marching south to counter this second invasion. To goad the Saxon King on, Norman soldiers burn Saxon estates.

Marauding across the hills and dales of southern England, the Normans loot Saxon farms. Under the watchful eye of a mounted knight dressed in chain mail, soldiers head back to their encampment with a grand array of livestock. With an ax raised high over his head, one man prepares to slaughter a sheep while another (far right) carries a pig to fatten the Normans' fare.

Preparing for battle, William dons his chain mail and Norman helmet and clutches his standard, preparatory to mounting the charger brought to him by a squire. William's well-rested troops were to face Harold's foot-weary army, which had to make a 65-mile march in three days to join in battle. The towers behind William signal a change in scene throughout the tapestry.

Trotting toward Senlac Hill, where Harold's army has arrived and claimed a dominant position, the Normans flaunt their cavalry. While the Saxon army —numbering 7,000 men— still fights on foot in the old Viking style with few archers, William's men will use more sophisticated battle techniques, alternating mass archery barrages with cavalry charges.

After being struck by a Norman arrow in the eye, brave Harold (far left) is hacked in two by a Norman knight on horseback wielding a broad sword. The Norman forces fought on until all those who were with the Saxon King had fallen. Later William of Poitiers was to write, "The bloodstained battleground was covered with the flower of the youth and nobility of England."

Approaching the battleground at the head of his horsemen (extreme right), William finds that the attack can only proceed up a gradual front slope because of the hill's steep sides. For hours his archers and cavalry batter the Saxon line. Then William has his army pretend to flee, luring the Saxons to chase them into a vale where the Norman soldiers turn and slaughter them.

The Bayeux Tapestry ends in tatters as William becomes master of England. The Latin inscription concludes: "The English have turned to flight" as heavily armed Norman cavalrymen pursue the weary survivors of King Harold's army. Duke William's campaign of brutal submission was to continue for the next five years and go down in history as "the harrying of the north."

Bibliography

Abbon, *Le Siege de Paris par les Normands* (edited and translated by Henri Waquet). Société d'Edition "Les Belles Lettres," 1942.

Almgren, Bertil, et al., *The Viking*. Tre Tryckare, Cagner, 1966.

Anderson, Joseph, ed., *The Orkneyinga Saga*. Merchat Press, 1977.

Arbman, Holger, *The Vikings*. Praeger, 1961.

Ashe, Geoffrey, *Land to the West*. Viking, 1962.

Backes, Magnus, and Regine Dölling, *Art of the Dark Ages*. Abrams, 1969.

Beowulf (translated by Lucien Dean Pearson). Indiana University Press, 1965.

Billington, James H., *The Icon and the Axe*. Knopf, 1966.

Boyer, Régis, *Le Livre de la Colonisation de L'Islande (Landnámabók)*. Mouton, 1973.

Bremen, Adam of, *History of the Archbishops of Hamburg-Bremen* (translated by Francis J. Tschan). Columbia University Press, 1959.

Brøgger, A. W., and Haakon Shetelig, *The Viking Ships: Their Ancestry and Evolution*. Twayne Publishers, 1971.

Brøndsted, Johannes, *The Vikings*. Penguin, 1965.

Brooke, Christopher, *From Alfred to Henry III 871-1272*. Thomas Nelson, 1961.

Campbell, Alistair, *Encomium Emmae Reginae*. Royal Historical Society, 1949.

Christensen, Arne Emil, Jr., *Boats of the North*. Det Norske Samlaget, 1968.

Clark, Anne, *Beasts and Bawdy*. Taplinger, 1975.

Crichton, Michael, *Eaters of the Dead*. Knopf, 1976.

Davidson, H. R. Ellis, *Gods and Myths of Northern Europe*. Penguin, 1964.

Dixon, Philip, *Barbarian Europe*. Phaidon, 1976.

Dolley, Michael, *Viking Coins of the Danelaw and Dublin*. British Museum, 1965.

Donovan, Frank R., *The Vikings*. American Heritage, 1964.

Egil's Saga (translated by E. R. Eddison). Cambridge University Press, 1930.

Egil's Saga (translated by Hermann Pálsson and Paul Edwards). Penguin, 1976.

Eirik the Red and Other Icelandic Sagas (translated by Gwyn Jones). Oxford University Press, 1961.

Elliott, Ralph W. V., *Runes*. Manchester University Press, 1971.

Enterline, James Robert, *Viking America*. Doubleday, 1972.

Foote, Peter G., and David M. Wilson, *The Viking Achievement*. Praeger, 1970.

Froncek, Thomas, *The Northmen*. The Emergence of Man. TIME-LIFE BOOKS, 1974.

Gad, Finn, *The History of Greenland*, Vol. I, *Earliest Times to 1700* (translated by Ernst Dupont). McGill-Queen's University Press, 1971.

Gordon, E. V., *The Battle of Maldon*. Methuen, 1937.

Haskins, Charles Homer, *The Normans in European History*. W. W. Norton, 1966.

Henry, Françoise, *Irish Art during the Viking Invasions*. Cornell University Press, 1967.

Hermannsson, Halldor, "Illuminated Manuscripts of the Jonsbok," *Islandica*, Vol. XXVIII. Cornell University Press, 1940.

Holand, Hjalmar R., *Norse Discoveries and Explorations in America, 982-1362*. Dover, 1969.

Hrafnkel's Saga (translated by Hermann Pálsson). Penguin, 1971.

Hughes, Kathleen, *Early Christian Ireland: Introduction to the Sources*. Cornell University Press, 1972.

Ingstad, Helge:
Land under the Pole Star. St. Martin's, 1966.
Westward to Vinland. St. Martin's, 1969.

Jansson, Sven B. F., *The Runes of Sweden*. Bedminster Press, 1962.

Jones, Gwyn:
A History of the Vikings. Oxford University Press, 1968.
The Norse Atlantic Saga. Oxford University Press, 1964.

Kendrick, T. D., *A History of the Vikings*. Scribner's, 1930.

Kennedy, Charles W., *Beowulf: the Oldest English Epic*. Oxford University Press, 1940.

The King's Mirror (translated by Laurence Marcellus Larson). American-Scandinavian Foundation, 1917.

Kirkby, Michael H., *The Vikings*. E. P. Dutton, 1977.

Klindt-Jensen, Ole, *The World of the Vikings*. Robert B. Luce, 1970.

Knuth, Egil, *Aron of Kangek: The Norsemen and the Skraelings*. Det Gronlandske Forlag, 1968.

Körner, Sten, *The Battle of Hastings, England, and Europe*. Skanska Centraltryckeriert, 1964.

Kristjánsson, Jónas, *Icelandic Sagas and Manuscripts*. Saga Publishing, 1970.

Krogh, Knud J., *Viking Greenland*. Copenhagen National Museum, 1967.

LaFay, Howard:
"The Vikings." *National Geographic Magazine*, Vol. 137, No. 4, Apr. 1970.
The Vikings. National Geographic Society, 1972.

Larson, Laurence M., *The Earliest Norwegian Laws*. Columbia University Press, 1935.

Laxdaela Saga (translated by Magnus Magnusson and Hermann Pálsson). Penguin, 1969.

Lewis, Archibald R., *The Northern Seas: Shipping and Commerce in Northern Europe, A.D. 300-1100*. Princeton University Press, 1958.

Loyn, H. R., *The Vikings in Britain*. St. Martin's Press, 1977.

Mackinlay, J. B., *Saint Edmund King and Martyr*. Art and Book, 1893.

MacManes, Seumas, *The Story of the Irish Race*. Devin-Adair, 1944.

Magnusson, Magnus:
Hammer of the North. Orbis, 1976.
Viking Expansion Westwards. Henry Z. Walck, 1973.

Marcus, G. J., "The Navigation of the Norsemen." *Mariner's Mirror*, Vol. XXXIX, No. 2, May 1953.

Morison, Samuel Eliot, *The European Discovery of America: The Northern Voyages, A.D. 500-1600*. Oxford University Press, 1971.

Musset, Lucien, *Les Invasions: Le Second Assaut contre l'Europe Chrétienne*. Presses Universitaires de France, 1971.

Nansen, Fridtjof, *In Northern Mists*, Vols. I and II. Stokes, 1911.

Nicolaysen, N., *The Viking Ship Discovered at Gokstad in Norway*. Cammermeyer, 1882.

Njal's Saga (translated by Magnus Magnusson and Hermann Pálsson). Penguin Books, 1960.

Nørlund, Paul, *Viking Settlers in Greenland*. Cambridge University Press, 1936.

Oxenstierna, Eric:
The Norsemen. New York Graphic Society, 1965.
The World of the Norsemen. The World Publishing Company, 1967.

Pohl, Frederick J., *The Viking Explorers*. Crowell, 1966.

Robertson, A. J., ed., *Laws of the Kings of England from Edmund to Henry I*. Cambridge University Press, 1925.

Rodgers, William L., *Naval Warfare under Oars*. U.S. Naval Institute, Annapolis, 1967.

The Russian Primary Chronicle, Laurentian Text (translated and edited by Samuel Hazzard Cross and Olgerd P. Sherbowitz-Wetzor). Crimson Printing Company, 1931.

The Saga of Grettir the Strong (translated by George Hight). Everyman, 1960.

Sawyer, P. H., *The Age of the Vikings*. St. Martin's Press, 1971.

Scherman, Katherine, *Daughter of Fire; A Portrait of Iceland*. Little, Brown, 1976.

Sellman, R. R., *The Vikings*. Roy Publishers, 1957.

Setton, Kenneth M., "900 Years Ago: The Norman Conquest." *National Geographic Magazine*, Vol. 130, No. 2, Aug. 1966.

Severin, Timothy, "The Voyage of 'Brendan'." *National Geographic Magazine*, Vol. 152, No. 6, Dec. 1977.

Simons, Gerald, *Barbarian Europe*. Great Ages of Man. TIME-LIFE BOOKS, 1968.

Simpson, Colin, *The Viking Circle*. Fielding Publications, 1966.

Simpson, Jacqueline, *Everyday Life in the Viking Age*. G. P. Putnam's Sons, 1967.

Sjovold, Thorhef, *The Oseberg Find and the Other Viking Ship Finds*. Universitetets Oldsaksamling, 1976.

Stenton, F. M.:
Anglo-Saxon England. Oxford University Press, 1975.
ed., *The Bayeux Tapestry*. Phaidon, 1957.

Stockholm Statens Historiska Museum, *The World of the Vikings*. National Maritime Museum, 1973.

Strayer, Joseph R., *Western Europe in the Middle Ages*. Appleton-Century-Crofts, 1955.

Sturlunga Saga (translated by Julia McGrew), 2 vols. Twayne Publishers, 1970.

Sturluson, Snorri:
From the Sagas of the Norse Kings (translated by Erling Monsen). Dreyers Forlag, 1967.
The Heimskringla, A History of the Norse Kings (translated by Samuel Laing). Norroena Society, 1906.
Heimskringla: The Norse King Sagas (translated by Samuel Laing). E. P. Dutton, 1951.

Sweeney, James J., *The Poetry of Vision*. Royal Dublin Society, 1971.

Treasures of Early Irish Art: 1500 B.C. to 1500 A.D. Metropolitan Museum of Art, 1977.

The Vatnsdaler Saga (translated by Gwyn Jones). Kraus Reprint Co., 1973.

Vernadsky, George:
Kievan Russia. Yale University Press, 1948.
The Origins of Russia. Clarendon, 1959.

The Vinland Sagas: The Norse Discovery of America (translated by Magnus Magnusson and Hermann Pálsson). Penguin Books, 1965.

Whitelock, Dorothy, ed., *The Anglo-Saxon Chronicle*. Rutgers University Press, 1961.

Wilson, David M., *The Vikings and Their Origins*. McGraw-Hill, 1970.

Wilson, David M., and Ole Klindt-Jensen, *Viking Art*. George Allen and Unwin, 1966.

Acknowledgments

The index for this book was prepared by Gale Partoyan. The editors wish to thank the following: John Batchelor, artist *(pages 79-81)*, Peter McGinn, artist *(end-paper maps)*, Richard Schlecht, artist, and William A. Baker, consultant *(pages 44-45, 60-65, 134-141)*, and Lloyd K. Townsend, artist *(cover, pages 47-51 and 99-101)*.

The editors also wish to thank: In Cardiff, Wales: Gwyn Jones, University College. In Copenhagen: Agnete Loth, Det Arnamagnaeanske Institut; Poul Mørk, The National Museum. In Edinburgh: David H. Caldwell, National Museum of Antiquities of Scotland. In Heidelberg: Wilfried Werner, Bibliotheksdirektor und Leiter der Handschrifenabteilung, Universität Heidelberg. In Italy: Antonietta Morandini, Director, Biblioteca Medicea-Laurenziana, Florence; His Eminence Antonio Cardinal Samorè, Director, Biblioteca Apostolica Vaticana, Rome; Gian Albino Ravalli-Modoni, Director, Biblioteca Nazionale Marciana, Venice. In London: Peter Clayton, Publications Department, Angela Evans and Daffyd Kidd, Department of Medieval and Later Antiquities, British Museum; Edward Telesford, British Museum Photographic Service; Peter Foote, University of London. Elsewhere in England: Terence Volk, Department of Coins and Medals, The Fitzwilliam Museum, Cambridge; Peter Sawyer, University of Leeds; R. I. H. Charlton, Publications Officer, Ashmolean Museum, Oxford. In Madrid: Manuel Carrion Gutiez, Vice Director, Biblioteca Nazional. In Moscow: Copyright Agency of the U.S.S.R. In Oslo: Arne Emil Christensen and Ove Holst, Universitetets Oldsaksamling. In Paris: François Avril, Curator, Département des Manuscrits, Bibliothèque Nationale. In Reykjavik: Kristjan Eldjarn, President, Republic of Iceland; Finnbogi Gudmundsson, Curator, Landsbókasafn Islands; Gudmundur Ólafsson, The National Museum; Stefán Karlsson, Jónas Kristjánsson, Curator, Einar Gunnar Pétursson, Stofnun Árna Magnússonar, Arnemagnaean Collection, University of Reykjavík. In Stockholm: Brigitte Straubinger, Antikvarisk Topografiska Arkivet, Statens Historiska Museum; Lena Thaalin-Bergman, Statens Historiska Museum. In Vienna: Robert Kittler, Oesterreichische Nationalbibliothek.

The editors also wish to thank: In Washington, D.C.: Peter Bell, Geophysical Laboratory, Carnegie Institution of Washington; Nils Toft, Cultural Attaché, Embassy of Denmark; Lars Tangeraas, Cultural Attaché, Embassy of Norway; David M. Goldfrank, Associate Professor of History, Director of Russian Area Studies, Georgetown University; Finn Henriksen, Senior Legal Specialist, European Law Division, Library of Congress; J. Lawrence Angel, Curator of Physical Anthropology, National Museum of Natural History, Smithsonian Institution. Elsewhere in the United States: Gabrielle Spiegel, Assistant Professor of History, University of Maryland, College Park; William Voelkle, Curator of Manuscripts, The Pierpont Morgan Library, New York; Robert H. Perry, Seattle.

Quotations from *The King's Mirror*, translated by Laurence M. Larson, were reprinted by permission of The American-Scandinavian Foundation, © 1917. Other particularly valuable sources were: *The Vikings* by Johannes Brøndsted, translated by Kalle Skov, Pelican Books, 1965, © Estate of Johannes Brøndsted; *The Norse Atlantic Saga* by Gwyn Jones, © Oxford University Press, 1964, reprinted by permission of Oxford University Press; *Aron of Kangek': The Norsemen and the Skraelings* by Eigil Knuth, The Greenlandic Publishing House, Godthaab, Greenland, © 1968.

Picture Credits

The sources for the illustrations in this book are shown below. Credits from left to right are separated by semicolons, from top to bottom by dashes.

Cover: Drawing by Lloyd K. Townsend. Front and back end papers: Drawing by Peter McGinn.

3: Universitetets Oldsaksamling, Oslo. 6 through 13: The Pierpont Morgan Library, New York. 14, 15: Derek Bayes, courtesy Department of the Environment, London. 16: Radio Times Hulton Picture Library, London. 18: By permission of the British Library. Cotton Tib Bv 56v. 21: Erich Lessing from Magnum, Paris, courtesy Nationalmuseet, Copenhagen. 22: Universitetets Oldsaksamling, Oslo. 23: Skira, Geneva, courtesy Church of Nea Moni, Chios, Greece; National Museum of Antiquities of Scotland, Edinburgh—Lennart Larsen, courtesy Nationalmuseet, Copenhagen. 24: The National Museum of Iceland, Reykjavik. 26, 27: Det Arnamagnaeanske Institut, Copenhagen. 30: Universitetets Oldsaksamling, Oslo; Lennart Larsen, courtesy Nationalmuseet, Copenhagen; Gabriel Hildebrand, courtesy Antikvarisk-Topografiska Arkivet (A.T.A.), Statens Historiska Museum, Stockholm. 31: Universitetets Oldsaksamling, Oslo; Lennart Larsen, courtesy Nationalmuseet, Copenhagen. 33: Det Arnamagnaeanske Institut, Copenhagen. 34, 35: Jac Brun, Mittet Foto A/S, courtesy Universitetets Oldsaksamling, Oslo. 36, 37: Universitetets Oldsaksamling, Oslo. 38: Universitetets Oldsaksamling, Oslo (2)—Jac Brun, Mittet Foto A/S, courtesy Universitetets Oldsaksamling, Oslo. 39: Jac Brun, Mittet Foto A/S, courtesy Universitetets Oldsaksamling, Oslo. 40, 41: Aldus Books, London, courtesy Arnamagnaen Collection, Aarhus, Denmark. 42: Studio 28, courtesy The Manuscript Institute, Reykjavik.

44: Drawing by Richard Schlecht. 45: Drawings by Richard Schlecht—Sören Hallgren, courtesy A.T.A., Statens Historiska Museum, Stockholm (2). 47 through 51: Drawings by Lloyd K. Townsend. 52: Studio 28, courtesy The Manuscript Institute, Reykjavik. 55: Lennart Larsen, courtesy Nationalmuseet, Copenhagen—Werner Forman Archive, London, courtesy Statens Historiska Museum, Stockholm. 56, 57: Jens-Joergen Frimand, courtesy Danmarks Kirker, Copenhagen. 59: Harald Faith-Ell, courtesy A.T.A., Statens Historiska Museum, Stockholm. 60 through 65: Drawings by Richard Schlecht. 66: Gabriel Hildebrand, courtesy A.T.A., Statens Historiska Museum, Stockholm. 68: Picture Collection, The New York Public Library, Astor, Lenox and Tilden Foundations. 71: Giraudon, courtesy Musée du Louvre, Paris. 72, 73: Réunion des Musées Nationaux, courtesy Cabinet des Dessins, Musée du Louvre, Paris. 74: Staatsbibliothek Preussischer Kulturbesitz, Berlin. M.Hamilton 150/1. 77: Courtauld Institute of Art, London, by permission of Master and Fellows of Corpus Christi College, Cambridge—courtesy The Ashmolean Museum, Oxford. 79, 80, 81: Drawings by John Batchelor. 83: Courtauld Institute of Art, London, by permission of the Master and Fellows of Corpus Christi College, Cambridge. 84: From *Codex Aureus*, courtesy Det Kungliga Bibliadeket, Stockholm. 85: Gabriel Hildebrand, courtesy A.T.A., Statens Historiska Museum, Stockholm; Universitetets Oldsaksamling, Oslo—Lennart Larsen, courtesy Nationalmuseet, Copenhagen. 87: Courtesy the British Museum. 88 through 93: Oleg Tsesarski, courtesy of the copyright agency of the U.S.S.R., Moscow, and the Library of the Academy of Sciences of the U.S.S.R., Leningrad. 94, 97: Gabriel Hildebrand, courtesy A.T.A., Statens Historiska Museum, Stockholm. 98, 99, 100:

Drawings by Lloyd K. Townsend. 102: Library of Congress. 105: Courtesy Museum of Fine Arts, Boston—Sören Hallgren, courtesy A.T.A., Statens Historiska Museum, Stockholm; Jan Nordqvist, courtesy Länsmuseet I Gävlesborg, Gävle, Sweden. 106: Harald Faith-Ell, courtesy A.T.A., Statens Historiska Museum, Stockholm. 108: Gabriel Hildebrand, courtesy A.T.A., Statens Historiska Museum, Stockholm. 109: Werner Forman Archive, London, courtesy Nationalmuseet, Copenhagen; Sören Hallgren, courtesy A.T.A., Statens Historiska Museum, Stockholm—Gabriel Hildebrand, courtesy A.T.A., Statens Historiska Museum, Stockholm (2). 110: Studio 28, courtesy The National Library of Iceland, Reykjavik. 112: Library of Congress. 115: Jac Brun, Mittet Foto A/S, courtesy Universitetets Oldsaksamling, Oslo. 116, 117: Myndidn, courtesy The National Library of Iceland, Reykjavik. 118: Courtesy The Manuscript Institute, Reykjavik. 121, 122, 123: Universitätsbibliothek Heidelberg. Cod.Pal. Germ.60. 124: Courtesy the British Museum. 128: Myndidn, courtesy The Manuscript Institute, Reykjavik. 131: Studio 28, courtesy The National Museum of Iceland, Reykjavik. 132: Courtesy Det Arnamagnaeanske Institut, Copenhagen. 134 through 141: Drawings by Richard Schlecht. 142: Courtesy Arnamagnaen Collection, Aarhus, Denmark. 144, 145: Biblioteca Medicea-Laurenziana, Florence. 147: Per Christoffersen, EGM-Foto, courtesy Riksarkivet, Oslo. 149, 150: Lennart Larsen, courtesy Nationalmuseet, Copenhagen. 152: Studio 28, courtesy The Manuscript Institute, Reykjavik. 155 through 158: Lennart Larsen, courtesy Etnografisk afd., Nationalmuseet, Copenhagen. 160: Bibliothèque Royale Albert I, Brussels. Ms 13076-77 Fol 24v. 162 through 169: With special authorization from the City of Bayeux.

Index